Enjoy the Book!

Tammy Larsen Esponge

Real Estate Disasters

Real Estate Disasters

A Post-Katrina Survival Guide
for Housing, Property and Insurance Catastrophes
by America's #1 Expert

Tammy Frosch Esponge

Adaly Publishing

Real Estate Disasters
Copyright © 2007 by Tammy Frosch Esponge
Published by Adaly Publishing

All rights reserved. No part of this book may be reproduced (except for inclusion in reviews), disseminated or utilized in any form or by any means, electronic or mechanical, including photocopying, recording, or in any information storage and retrieval system, or the Internet/World Wide Web without written permission from the author or publisher.

This book is intended for a general audience, does not purport to give legal advice and is not intended as a substitute for professional assistance and therefore no individual should undertake the recommendations contained herein without careful study and critical consideration. The author and publisher make no warranties or representation as to the effectiveness of the suggestions contained herein for specific readers and their specific situations. Because no two situations may be the same, and it is recommended to always consult with professionals. The publisher and author disclaim any responsibility for adverse affects resulting directly or indirectly from information contained herein.

For further information, please contact:

Tammy Frosch Esponge
1615 Ellerslie Avenue
La Place, LA 70068
email at aagno@bellsouth.net

Printed in the United States of America

Real Estate Disasters
Tammy Frosch Esponge

1. Title 2. Author 3. Disaster Relief/Hurricane Katrina

Library of Congress Control Number: 2006939558

ISBN-10: 0-9789178-1-2
ISBN-13: 978-0-9789178-1-4

Table of Contents

Introduction vii

Chapter One 1

Chapter Two 19

Chapter Three 33

Chapter Four 43

Chapter Five 53

Chapter Six 69

Chapter Seven 79

Chapter Eight 91

Chapter Nine 103

Chapter Ten 125

Introduction

Katrina was the costliest hurricane in the history of the United States, both financially and in terms of lives lost. She devastated cities along the coasts of Alabama Mississippi and Louisiana, causing over $80 billion in damage and killing more than a thousand people Louisiana alone.

Two thousand people died overall, and unbelievable as it may seem, we're still finding bodies in the ruins of New Orleans. Eighteen thousand businesses were destroyed. Roads, schools, public facilities and medical services were wiped out. Thousands of people became refugees overnight.

The devastation to owner-occupied homes was unprecedented, with 122,000 either flattened or suffering major damage. The same was true of rental properties, where something like 84,000 were destroyed. Some estimates put repair costs to residential properties at $32 billion—much of it not covered by insurance. A substantial portion of the units that are now uninhabitable was at the time occupied by low-income households.

As terrible as all this was, it was followed by even more devastation when hurricane Rita rolled in on September 24, 2005. Rita was in fact a stronger storm, breaking the record Katrina had just set for the strongest hurricane ever recorded in the Gulf of Mexico. If she'd followed Katrina's path, we probably wouldn't have a city anymore.

But she didn't. She just rolled on by, catching us with her edge—enough to cause major flooding again, but not enough to flatten the Big Easy. So that was a bullet we dodged.

Talk to government officials and they'll tell you about how much money was raised for the relief effort. The U.S. Department of Housing and Urban Development's Community Development Block Grant Program provided $11.5 billion to the states of Mississippi, Louisiana, Alabama, Florida and Texas, $6.2 billion of which went to Louisiana alone; there's another $4.2 billion in resources pending appropriation by Congress. From Capitol Hill, there's a temptation to see the problem in terms of numbers.

Talk to the man on the street, or the woman who watched the tragedy unfold live on TV, and they will tell you that Katrina was about the people who had to run (or swim) from their homes as the storm raged above them, or the people who sheltered as a last resort in the Superdome, without sanitation or light.

Faced with so much tragedy, few people think about the owners of rental properties that were left standing empty as the levees collapsed and the tenants left town. After all, those owners weren't losing their lives; they weren't even losing the roofs over their own heads, were they?

No. Generally speaking, they were not. But they were still in a fight for survival as their headquarters were destroyed and their employees were scattered across the state. They also had to watch as rotting carpet and furniture, moldy refrigerators and stagnant water destroyed assets they had spent years, in some case lifetimes, building up.

Not many people think about the owners, but I do. I work for and with them, trying to help where I can in defending their interests, or offering guidance and advice. In the aftermath of Katrina, my description changed a little; standing up to my knees in dirty water, helping a man drag a departed tenant's furniture into a pile in the middle of the room because legislation wouldn't *allow* him to throw it out into the street, I got a different perspective on the whole thing.

It was a viewpoint that broadened over months of trying to help owners and tenants put their lives back together against a backdrop of administrative blunders, frustrating legislation, insurance Catch 22s and local politics. Because the story of Katrina is not just the story of a storm and a city that was built too close to the water. It is the story of a community at odds with its government, both local and federal; the story of a community at odds with itself.

In the past year or so, many people here have come to the view Katrina as only partly a natural disaster. They say that what happened to the city was a catastrophe made in Washington.

In its simplest form, this argument states that the Army Corps of Engineers constructed barriers—*levees*, to use the proper term—that were inadequate for the job. Specialists say that had the levees been built right, the water would never have flooded the city.

This argument also states that the government employed the army, so the government should pick up the tab. For *everything*. Every house, whether it was inside the flood plain or out, insured or uninsured. The government let this city sprawl the way it sprawled, the government let this city think it was safe when it wasn't. So the government is to blame.

Others say that the people are to blame—the people in the Ninth Ward, for example, who have been living in the floodplain for generations without adequate insurance or structural precautions that would alleviate the effect of a flood.

As you can probably imagine, a climate that allows arguments like that to flourish is a political climate, a politicized climate, and there is no doubt that a large part of what has happened to New Orleans since August 26, 2005 has been skewed by, shaped by and in the last analysis, hampered by politics.

But it is not my intention in this book to take a political line, or to point fingers for the sake of pointing; because at a certain level, I firmly believe that no one group is totally to blame (even if the Army Corps of Engineers comes pretty close). In a significant sense, this city just happened, like most cities just happen—evolving over time, changing with the decades, always in the process of becoming something else.

When the French first founded New Orleans, they chose the location because of its relative elevation above land that was susceptible to flooding along the banks of the Mississippi. In other words, the first piece of urban planning was rational and perfectly valid.

What happened later, when the city was allowed to sprawl out from the high ground and the natural levees into lower lying areas, was maybe not so smart, but there again, it was based on the rational assumption that water could be pumped out of those areas. As for the fact that an awful lot of the city is below sea level—that is something that developed over the course of the 20th century, partly due to man, partly due to nature.

So if you want to read a book about politics in the Big Easy, you should probably look somewhere else. But if you want to read about what happens when a city falls apart, street by street, apartment building by apartment building, and what happens when a variety of authorities and local players come to together to try to fix it, then this is a book you'll find interesting. If you want to know what it was like to be there, and to be dealing with the aftermath of a catastrophe on a daily basis, then this is the book for you.

I work for the Apartment Association of Greater New Orleans and Louisiana, and I learned some lessons down there in the flooded streets of East New Orleans—hard lessons about the price you can pay by not being prepared for a major catastrophe, whether it be a Category 5 storm or an earthquake.

These lessons were confirmed and compounded in the

months that followed the storm, as I sat through meetings with FEMA officials who were trying to get a handle on what turned out to be one of the biggest cans of worms you could ever imagine; or as I watched as the mayor and the governor tried to come up with a plan for a community that was deeply divided before Katrina, and which now saw all its divisions revealed.

Reed Kroloff, the architecture dean at Tulane University, which happens to be the city's biggest employer, was one of the first people Mayor Ray Nagin invited to come up with a plan to rebuild after Katrina. Rebuilding is something Kroloff knows all about, and not just from an academic perspective: two-thirds of the Tulane campus was flooded by Katrina and the university has spent almost $200 million restoring buildings since that happened.

They also cut hundreds of jobs, including the entire engineering school, and purchased and rented housing to accommodate displaced faculty and students. They then persuaded about three-quarters of the student body to return to the city.

In other words, they did in miniature what the governor, the mayor and the administration have been trying to do for New Orleans as a whole. Tulane did it, and they did it well, which is why it is interesting when Dean Kroloff gives his opinion on the recovery effort. This is his opinion: it was, he says, "the perfect storm of bad policy."

This is the story of that storm. And the one that came before it.

CHAPTER ONE

The Coming Storm

There's a saying: life is what happens when you're planning something else.

Thinking about it later, I came to see how much Friday, August 26, 2005 was a prime example of exactly that: me planning away furiously and then life taking a hand. I was planning, planning, planning—thinking about the coming weekend, up to my ears in various projects at work. You know how it is.

I work for the Apartment Association of Greater New Orleans and Louisiana, serving more than a hundred owners who in turn rent upwards of 25,000 units to something like 60,000 people. So you can bet your bottom dollar that I'm always pretty busy—and at that time of the year, particularly so.

The Association was building up to its annual conference, due to take place on September 16, and I was taking in registration forms and contacting people, talking to attendees about their hotel reservations, finalizing matters with the speakers and so on. On top of that, the New Orleans Apartment Association was preparing for its end-of-the-year banquet along with the presentation of awards for excellence, which was to happen at the beginning of November.

To cap it all, I'd been working hard to prepare for the 40th wedding anniversary of my in-laws, who lived out in Buras, Louisiana, which is on that little piece of the state that dangles out there in the Gulf, the first place to get evacuated in case of an incoming storm…

It's almost funny to think of it now: I was working the phones, immersed in the day-to-day running of the office, while out there in the Gulf, this enormous primal thing was gathering force.

Poor Katrina. She probably didn't mean any harm. She just didn't know her own strength. By that time, she'd only been alive for a couple of days; she came into being over the southeastern Bahamas, the spawn of a tropical wave and the remains of "Tropical Depression 10"—or so the papers later said.

They named her on the morning of August 24, when she got big enough and angry enough to be called a tropical storm, and then she was really rolling—not yet a hurricane, only getting that nasty on August 24th, when they named her Katrina and she headed straight for Florida.

Or so we thought. We thought, "Poor Florida. Not again." That was the refrain I heard in the few phone calls I had that day that mentioned the storm at all. By then, Katrina had already taken a little nibble at the Sunshine State—putting out the lights for a lot of people, causing between $1 and $2 billion worth of damage. That was nothing for this gal, even as the lowly Category 1 storm she was at that stage!

But she'd done harm already, and Jeb Bush thought she might do more. So he declared a state of emergency and was closing down schools and opening up shelters. And we were watching all this—to the extent that we were watching at all—and thinking, "Okay, so it's happening over there, right? Katrina is going to turn and head up into the Panhandle, right?"

Wrong.

She didn't do that. She kind of rolled on out into the Gulf and just got stronger and deeper and meaner and faster, picking up energy over the warm waters, looking for somewhere else to visit, somewhere no big storm had been in a while...

Meanwhile, I was on the phone making plans. I had conferences to organize, plus a banquet and a wedding anniversary. I guess, in a way, I was like everyone else: I'd been lulled into a false sense of security. I mean, we hadn't been hit by a big storm in over 40 years. So what if we lived in the third lowest place in the United States, right up there (or down there, I guess you'd have to say) with Death Valley and the Salton Sea? So what if over half of the city was actually below sea level?

If you look at a cross-section of the city, the masses of water that are Lake Pontchartrain and the Mississippi look—well, there's no other word for it: threatening. Billions of tons of water, stood up on either side of the city like when Moses split the Red Sea, and the only things holding that water back were some levees—these skinny little walls of dirt and concrete.

We are surrounded by water, and in many places, we live on top of it. This is why most houses in the city do not have basements. This is why the crypts in the cemeteries are built above ground.

The city is in fact located in what is known as the Mississippi Alluvial Plain, kind of squeezed in between the river to the south and the lake to the north. The only way it stays dry is by having rainwater pumped into Lake Pontchartrain through a system of canals that are contained by levees, dikes and floodwalls—which are all different names for basically the same thing: barriers. We live behind these barriers, and pretty much always have, ever since the first artificial levees and canals that were built in early colonial times.

Back then, flooding from lake Pontchartrain was rare and never that serious because most of the old town was constructed on high ground along the riverfront and showed its back to the lake and the swampy ground around it. But as the city grew and demand for land increased, people started building lower down and so inevitably, flooding started to be more of a problem.

As a result, a lot of the buildings that went up in the 19th century were raised at least a foot above street level, and often several feet in order to allow for the fairly frequent flooding, which was just accepted as the price you paid for living closer to the water.

Simple, right? It's called going with the flow.

But it wasn't quite good enough, apparently. In the early 19th century, engineers started to get ideas about how to make the city really dry, starting with an ambitious system of underground drainage canals that ran beneath the streets. The basic idea was to drain water by gravity into the low-lying swamps and then supplement this with canals and mechanical pumps, which were powered by steam engine and started out by pushing water along the Orleans Canal out to Bayou St John.

Then, in 1859, a surveyor by the name of Louis H. Pilié set to work on improving the drainage canals by lining some portions with brick. By 1871, there were 36 miles of canals in the city. New Orleans started to look like the city we know.

But even then, it wasn't uncommon for the streets to be awash after heavy rain. Sometimes they stayed that way for days. You would have thought the city's fathers might have learned their lesson, but in fact, they were only just getting started with their improvements and in 1893, the Drainage Advisory Board came into being.

This led in turn to the Sewerage & Water Board, which took on the huge task of not only draining the city, but also building a modern sewerage and installing a tap water system. It was the Sewerage & Water Board that found a young engineer by the name of A. Baldwin Wood, and it was A. Baldwin Wood who pretty much single-handedly made the city what it is today.

Wood came up with a number of improvements for pumps and plumbing, and he pushed New Orleans into the era of massive drainage, making it pretty much as it is today—at least in terms of what happens to the water after it runs down your plughole.

If there were a moment in the city's history that you could point the finger of blame at, this was it. Baldwin's "improvement" filled the city with new confidence about what exactly was possible, and inevitably, a lot of land that had previously been swamp or used only as cow pasture was drained and then developed.

The city had completed it transformation, moving away from the higher ground close to the river and settling into areas that, while not at that time below sea level, were nevertheless very low lying.

What came next was a series of lessons for anyone inclined to pay attention and learn. In 1927, the city was flooded by a downpour of some 15 inches of rain falling in the space of 19 hours, which knocked out the municipal electricity system and stopped the pumping system cold.

It was also in 1927 that the project to build a more extensive system of levees on the shoreline of Lake Pontchartrain was started, which led in turn to the gradual development of the land around the lake. By 1945, there were houses right up to the edge of it.

We were getting closer and closer to the dragon's lair…

In 1947, there were more floods and more lessons when the Fort Lauderdale Hurricane slammed straight into the city, testing Wood's improved drainage pumps to the limit. They proved up to the task, but Jefferson Parish, which did not have the pumping system, disappeared under 6 feet of water.

In 1965, another hurricane—Betsy this time, and once again the city came through with flying colors, except for the Lower Ninth Ward.

And here, the lesson of history is pretty chilling. The Lower Ninth Ward, which is separated from the rest of the city by the Industrial Canal and the Gulf Intracoastal Waterway, was flooded not by rainfall, but by a levee breach—to be precise, a breach in the Industrial Canal levee, which resulted in catastrophic flooding and loss of life.

Sound familiar? It should.

Rather than change the fundamentals of the system, the city installed new pumping stations and by 1980, we had 20 of them running 89 pumps, which had a combined capacity of 15,642,000 gallons per minute, a flow that is comparable to the Ohio River.

And once again, mother nature tried to give us a lesson. This time, one that is within living memory for a lot of people. In May 1995, torrential rain overwhelmed pumping capacity once again and flooded vast swaths of the city, destroying houses and totaling huge numbers of cars.

This prompted a smattering of projects to increase drainage capacity in the worst hit areas. In other words, the city responded not by changing any of the fundamentals of the urban design, but by—you guessed it, installing more pumps.

By early 2005, the year Katrina came calling, we had 148 drainage pumps and felt like we were ready for anything.

But we weren't.

We weren't ready at all. All we'd done was buy ourselves a little denial time, a little space in which to ignore the simple fact that we were a very low-lying city, surrounded by water and stuck in the middle of Tropical-Storm-Six-Lane-Highway-One.

And I haven't even mentioned the coastal wetlands! That was something else we should have been worrying about—this natural barrier protecting us from incoming storms, which had been eroding for years and was by 2005 looking pretty threadbare.

According to the U.S. Geological Survey, material equivalent to a chunk of land about half the size of Rhode Island has vanished since the 1970s. What's worse is that our precious levee system—the thing we think makes us safe—is one of the reasons the wetlands are melting away.

It worked like this: the Mississippi carried huge amounts of sediment down from the Midwest and dumped it into the Gulf of Mexico, pushing the river mouth further and further into sea. A barrier was formed.

What the levees did was channel the river, preventing it from depositing sediment, which Ol' Miss finally dumped much further out—straight over the edge of the continental shelf, in fact. In this way, a barrier was not formed.

Meanwhile, Louisiana's oil and gas infrastructure—miles of pipelines and navigation channels—sliced into the coastal wetlands, bringing the saltwater inland and killing the plants that made the roots that prevented the wetlands from washing away. Our biggest barrier was all but gone. But we either didn't notice, or didn't care.

We were living in denial—or maybe we were just thinking about something else. And business was great, after all. The apartment industry had been on a roll for such a long, long time. Why would you want to look past that, to history's harsh lessons? Why would you think all that good stuff was coming to an end anytime soon?

We got the first sense that it might on Friday night, when things started to veer just a little off center. I got a phone call from my sister-in-law, saying that Plaquemines Parish, which was where my in-laws Terry and Lillie lived, was being evacuated. They said that in fact, there was a mandatory evacuation going on, and that the couple would be out of there by Saturday morning.

She said, "they're packing their bags, what are we going to do?" She wasn't worried about the hurricane. She was worried about Terry and Lillie's anniversary party.

It probably seems crazy to you. I mean there was this giant tropical buzz saw heading straight for the city, and all we could think about was the hall we had rented for the reception, the decorations, the food, the drinks; not to mention all the hard work we'd done to collect old pictures of Terry and Lillie going back over 40 years of marriage.

But that's how it is when you plan stuff: you lose perspective. And beyond that, there was the question of denial. I really didn't want to believe that the storm was just going to keep coming; I had convinced myself that it was going to turn away at the last moment.

But at least I was watching it then. Okay, I knew that they always evacuated Plaquemines Parish first, but still…Katrina had my attention. She had everyone's attention. She was doing interesting stuff. The weather people and hurricane watchers were talking about an "eyewall replacement cycle," which was disrupting her spin but making her bigger; in fact, she was doubling in size and then spinning faster again, intensifying.

And records were being broken. She was at that point the most powerful hurricane ever recorded in the Gulf of Mexico.

And maybe if I'd really been paying attention, I'd have just jumped into the car with the kids, but I went to bed Friday night thinking (okay, maybe "praying" is the word I want here) that Katrina would just pass us by.

Saturday went along in pretty much the same way—hot and humid with me in a state of anxiety, numbed partly by the anesthetic of denial. Katrina was making steady progress across the Gulf, getting upgraded to a Category 3. I didn't know it at the time, but Governor Blanco was already requesting federal assistance, telling the White House that there was no way the state could handle what was coming our way.

The White House bounced right back, authorizing FEMA to "identify, mobilize and provide at its discretion, equipment and resources necessary to alleviate the impacts of the emergency." Snappy communications were going back and forth, but as we later came to realize, not a whole lot was getting done.

I went to bed Saturday night pretty much as I had the night before: just praying for Katrina to pass us by. But out there in the Gulf, she just kept on coming, sucking up heat, getting faster until at 2:00 Sunday morning, when she was upgraded by the weather people to a Category 4.

Sunday morning, I was up at six. I didn't know it at the time, but Katrina was just an hour away from reaching her maximum intensity, and she was still barreling straight toward us. But there we were—a family with our cereal bowls and our morning routines, getting ready for the day.

My husband is a police officer and he had to go on duty, leaving me there at the house with my children, my parents and their dog. My sister was also there, as was her husband and their children, plus a friend of mine who is also married to a policeman.

I decided that we needed to move. Maybe I just ran out of denial and finally let myself hear or see what was going on around me. Maybe I caught a radio station talking about the emergency measures that were being taken. By then, 11 counties and 11 cities had issued evacuation orders, and people were on the move.

They'd opened 57 emergency shelters in coastal communities and said that they had another 31 available if needed. I guess that all filtered through at some point. Or maybe it was CNN saying that Katrina had just been upgraded to a Category 5, and I'd heard that magical number just once too often.

Earthquakes get Richter ratings; for storms, the scale was established by a character called Herbert Saffir. This isn't something I'd ordinarily know, but in those days of the gathering storm, we were all getting more knowledgeable about Katrina and her kin.

Ironically, Saffir came up with his scale while carrying out a study for the United Nations, looking into low-cost housing in hurricane-prone areas. I mean, he could have been describing certain parts of New Orleans! Saffir said that once winds got up to 156 miles per hour, you could expect "complete roof failure" on residences and industrial buildings, and some building "failures."

By that point, Katrina was reaching speeds up to 175 miles per hour—buzz saw fast. Under that kind of pressure, there was a serious concern that houses would just start to disintegrate and blow away.

But I think the real fear at the back of everyone's mind was what Katrina might do to the water, and what the water might do to the city.

By August 28, that Sunday when we were finally deciding to clear out, the "experts" were already running computer models showing that Katrina's right front quadrant (yes, this lady led with her right) could produce a surge as high as 28 feet. So, despite what the president later said about the levees, as early as Sunday the 28th, the emergency management officials knew there was a real concern about flooding.

In fact, there had been studies by FEMA and the Army Corps of Engineers that had raised the possibility of massive flooding should New Orleans ever take a direct hit. Also, as far back as 2001, the *Houston Chronicle* published a story which predicted that a severe hurricane hitting New Orleans square-on would likely strand 250,000 people or more, and probably kill one in ten left behind as the city disappeared under 20 feet of water. The *Chronicle* also predicted the flow of thousands of refugees to Houston.

So everyone knew about the risks. It wasn't even about whether the levees would breach or not; the idea was that the water might just come over the top.

I just started making phone calls (yep, making plans again). I got confirmed reservations at the Days Inn in Oxford Mississippi, then received an email telling us that they were overbooked and were putting us into a Super 8. "Wherever, whatever" was how we felt by that time, and we just got into our cars and headed out.

We got onto the contra-flow, which we rode in the opposite direction, and then took the I-55 all the way from Louisiana and up through Mississippi, getting to Oxford in about 5 and a half hours, which was your typical drive time for that run.

During the drive, Ray Nagin came on the radio ordering the first ever mandatory evacuation of the city. I remember him saying at one point that Katrina might just be "the storm that most of us have long feared."

Driving into Oxford, I felt pretty glad to have at least put some space between me and all that was about to happen in New Orleans. In fact, all in all, it was going relatively smoothly, given the circumstances, until I realized that I didn't have any money.

You kind of need money, preferably cash, when a city starts to fall apart, especially when you've got kids to feed. The Association is a non-profit organization, and I'm the only paid employee in the office, so I contacted one of our board members and worked something out whereby I would use the Association's debit account to pay myself while I was evacuating. I was planning on the run now, keeping just a couple of paces ahead of the disaster.

All this time, I was in contact with my husband and he was able to keep me up to date with what was going on in the area, which was basically the three-phase evacuation plan that had long been in place.

One of the big problems they had was that the private care-giving facilities, which depended on bus companies and ambulances to get people out, were stuck without rides. There wasn't much gasoline on sale, most of the rental cars had been taken and public transportation had all been shut down. It was of course a huge problem that ended up causing a great deal of suffering.

In the afternoon, we heard what was just a chilling hurricane warning, issued by the National Weather Service. They basically said that in the event of a Category 4 or 5 hurricane hitting the city, at least one-half of the homes would suffer roof failure and all gabled roofs would fail.

I had visions of my house opening up like a can of sardines and all the furniture being sucked out, but I tried to focus on the positive. I mean, we were all still alive and everyone except for our husbands were pretty much out of harm's way. So we thanked heaven for small mercies and settled in for another night.

Meanwhile, just a couple hundred miles away, the people who had been unable to get out of the city—a lot of them from homes managed by our members—were already cramming into the Louisiana Superdome, which had been chosen as the evacuation of last resort.

Then Monday morning came.

We were up at six a.m. I turned on the TV straight away to try to find out what had happened. And miracle of miracles, all the national media said that New Orleans had been spared once again. Talk about sighs of relief. It seemed too good to be true. After all the anxiety of the previous day, I thought, could it be that everything was going to be alright?

We went out to get some air, leaving my father behind at the motel. And I guess it was while we were out that Katrina, after her long journey across the Caribbean and into the Gulf (downgraded to a Category 4 and then a 3, but still spinning at a 125 miles per hour as she ripped into the city) finally made landfall.

Category 3 or not, she was still one very angry hurricane, gutting the upper floors of the high buildings in her path, ripping out the windows on the north side of the Hyatt Regency, sucking beds out into the screaming air, tearing at the roof of the Superdome, whirling her skirt of torrential rain.

As she rolled into New Orleans, she deposited up to 15 inches of rain in some places, swelling Lake Pontchartrain until it flooded along its northeastern shore, inundating the communities of Slidell and Mandeville, pulling apart bridges, including the I-10 twin span.

Almost immediately, there were reports of levees being breached. The Mississippi River Gulf Outlet, "MR-GO" as it is known locally, broke through its levees in 20 places, flooding much of New Orleans East, the majority of Saint Bernard Parish and the East Bank of Plaquemines Parish.

The most serious levee failures in the city included breaches at the London Avenue Canal and the wider, navigable Industrial Canal—which breached in three places, once on the upper side near the junction with MR-GO and twice on the lower side, along the Lower Ninth Ward between Florida Avenue and Claiborne Avenue.

The Lower Ninth Ward took the brunt of the flooding, the pumping stations there failing under the pressure so that by 11:00 that morning, the water stood 8 feet deep. In the late morning, a huge chunk of the 17th Street Canal levee gave way where it connected with the supposedly "hurricane proof" Old Hammond Highway bridge, and the water just gushed through.

The often-repeated lesson of history was being taught once again.

Of course, we were oblivious to all this. We were out taking our walk, planning our return, marveling at our good luck...

In the end, something like 80 percent of the city flooded.

And people were just stunned. It just didn't seem possible that the city's defenses could fail so comprehensively. At first, experts speculated that the storm surge had just come over the top of the levees, but then in the weeks that followed, as engineers started looking into it, this was found to be unlikely in the majority of cases, although it certainly happened and was even witnessed.

In the end, investigations were carried out by the Army Corps of Engineers and the American Society of Civil Engineers, which in a preliminary report concluded that the flooding in the Lakeview neighborhood was the result of the soil in the levees giving way.

There was apparently evidence that a section of the levee embankment that supported the actual floodwall had moved sideways—had been *pushed* sideways by the raging water, moving approximately 45 feet. There was also similar evidence of the dirt levee moving at the London Avenue breach.

Soil borings taken from the area of the 17th Street Canal breach revealed a layer of peat which started about 15 to 30 feet below the surface and made a layer between 5 and 20 feet thick.

When I first read about that layer of peat, which by all accounts is what's left of the old swamp on that area of New Orleans near Lake Pontchartrain, I couldn't help thinking back to the way the city used to be before all the improvements were made. It seemed as though we had built our castle—if not on sand, at least on mud.

Professor Robert Bea, a geotechnical engineer from UC Berkeley, said that this layer of peat had a very low shear strength and would make the base of any floodwall extremely susceptible to the stresses of a large flood.

"At 17th Street, the soil moved laterally, pushing entire wall sections with it," his report said.

Of course, once these finding emerged, everyone started looking at the way the levees had been built. The Army Corps of Engineers said that they had sunk their pilings 17 feet into the subsoil, but then a forensic engineering team from Louisiana State University used sonar to show that at a certain point near the 17th Street Canal breach, the piling extended just 10 feet below sea level.

Ten feet. Not 17, like the army said. The Louisiana State people were pretty clear about it: 10 feet was just not deep enough. Other reports confirmed that construction on the London Avenue and Industrial Canal levees also fell short of the Corps' *stated* standards.

It also turned out that there had been a chilling precursor to what happened on August 29th. Homeowners along the 17th Street Canal near the site of the breach had been reporting seepage from the canal flooding into their yards for a year prior to Katrina. Technically speaking, the levee was already breached.

In the months that followed, the picture only got worse. There were more studies, more damning conclusions until finally, at the Senate Committee on November 2, 2005, Ivor van Heerden from Louisiana State University concluded that most of the flooding of New Orleans was due to people screwing up.

"Society owes those who lost their lives, and the approximately 100,000 families who lost all, an apology, and needs to step up to the plate and rebuild their homes, and compensate for their lost means of employment", he said.

It was a message we all heard loud and clear. Incredibly, it wasn't until April 5, 2006, that Lieutenant General Carl Strock testified before the U.S. Senate Subcommittee on Energy and Water that there were problems with the design of the levee structure.

He also testified that the U.S. Army Corps of Engineers did not know of this mechanism of failure prior to Katrina, a claim which was later refuted by National Science Foundation investigators. On June 1st, 2006, the Corps finally admitted responsibility for what happened that morning in New Orleans.

It gives me chills now to think about it: us on our walk as all those centuries of great ideas and fine planning, combined with a few badly made walls, brought the whole city to its knees, drowning a lot of people along the way. It's hard not to see the disaster as some kind of judgment.

But as I say, we knew nothing about any of this, and when we got back to the motel a couple of hours later, we were surprised to find my father waiting for us stern-faced. He told us the new news: the city was drowning.

As for Katrina, she just kept on coming, tracking north until she rolled right over us, knocking out our power and sending us scurrying for cover. I guess that was as near as I got to feeling the anguish of those people left in the city: sitting there in the dark that night, surrounded by family and my friend whose husband was also a policeman down there in New Orleans, doing his job, as was mine.

We were completely cut off. We had no idea what was going on. We didn't say it, but we were wondering if we'd ever see our husbands or our homes again.

But guess what? Our Tuesday morning turned out better than most people's. My friend was able to contact her husband and he told us that not only was he okay, but so were our homes. In fact, they had suffered minimal damage and no flooding.

Which of course felt like an incredible blessing as we sat there watching people being rescued from rooftops on TV. And Katrina? Well, she finally ran out of gas somewhere over Jackson, Mississippi, where she just blended in as part of the weather. She lived a short life and brought a lot of misery—in the end killing over 2,000 people, leaving 3 million more without electricity, trashing houses and apartment buildings, and turning out to be the costliest natural disaster in the history of the United States.

And then, we had to clean up the mess.

CHAPTER TWO

Aftermath

Anyone who watched the TV coverage of the disaster probably thinks he or she has a pretty good idea of what went on in the following days. But I'm here to tell you, unless you were there looking at it, and maybe above all smelling it, as I did over the following days and weeks, you have no way of knowing how it really was.

By Tuesday, August 30th, when we were trying to decide what to do next, things had started to get really ugly in New Orleans as looting rapidly spread throughout the city. This was particularly scary for me, since my husband was out there in the thick of it.

He said that fires were starting up all over and the bad guys were roaming free, often armed, taking advantage of the fact that law enforcement was being assigned to rescue operations. It was happening everywhere, but focused on areas where there weren't many permanent residents, such as Lakeview and Gentilly.

The crooks were just walking right up and smashing store windows, and helping themselves to TVs and iPods and God knows what else, often in broad daylight. And of course, when the police tried to intervene, people complained that they were abandoning the victims of the storm. What people didn't seem to realize was that with only 1,500 policemen for the whole city, there was a limit to what they could do!

Of course, not everyone was stealing for the fun of it, of course. Many residents were just desperately struggling for survival, gathering food, water and other essentials wherever they could find them.

But for every starving victim of the storm it seemed like there were 10 bad guys, and I mean *really* bad. One of the most shocking incidents in those first days after the storm was the shooting on Danziger Bridge, where police opened fire on people who were (and this is hard to get your head round) shooting at soldiers with the Army Corps of Engineers, who were struggling to repair the 17th Street Canal.

Not quite as outrageous, but shocking to me all the same, was when the Tulane University medical center came under attack. Armed looters went there in boats, looking to load up with meds, I guess, and were driven back by the hospital staff.

The CEO of Acadian Ambulance Services appeared on CNN saying that if they didn't have a federal presence in New Orleans by dark, it would no longer be safe to be there, hospital or no hospital.

As bad as all this was, I think the thing that really grabbed our attention was what was happening in the Superdome—not because it was where the worst things happened (although a number of very bad things did) but because it was the place the local authorities had made available for people to take shelter from the storm. It was where people were supposed to be *safe*.

In the end, it came down to there being just too many people, I guess. Any plan the authorities had put together was overwhelmed by this tide of devastated, bedraggled people, carrying the few things that were left to them, shuffling into the dome. Sections of the roof had been damaged in the storm and on top of that, Katrina had basically ripped off the building's waterproofing. Because of the power outage, the dome's cooling system shut down pretty much from the get-go.

Now, the Superdome is in the business district and it can get pretty hot down there—and the humidity can be stifling. On top of everything else, on that first terrible Monday night, those people were there without light for a lot of the time. For a while, they had an emergency generator and when that gave out, engineers had to swim underwater to knock a hole in a wall to put in a new diesel line. Then the backup generator failed, and they were in the dark.

And the people just kept coming…

By Tuesday morning, reports were starting to emerge that there was a bad situation developing there, and by the end of that day, we heard that between 15,000 and 20,000 had gathered inside. Of course, the true horror of what was going on didn't emerge until later.

The situation overall in the city was so terrible—with 80,000 people estimated stranded, people being rescued off their rooftops and so forth—it was hard to focus on any one thing.

For us, stuck in the motel watching it all unfold, there was nothing to do but pack up and get back into our cars. We'd gotten word that our houses were fine, so it seemed like the most logical thing was to head back to our hometown of Laplace, which is located between Baton Rouge and New Orleans, a couple of miles west of Lake Pontchartrain.

When I told my husband about our plan to go back, he was less than thrilled; he wanted me to stay put. But to be perfectly honest, we were worried about looters. There had already been all these reports of looting and we wanted to get back just to make sure our homes were safe.

And I had other reasons to worry about looters. The thing was, the police had closed the city prior to the storm hitting, and by the time I'd realized what was really happening, I'd been unable to get back into the Apartment Association office to grab all the credit cards, check books and paperwork.

I didn't know it at the time, but several of my owners had been caught the same way. HRI, for example, which has buildings and hotels in the city, had cleared out on Friday, not expecting to see the city get hit. But it had and so had we all, and so on top of all the other things I'd been praying for in the past 48 hours, there was another: please don't let the Apartment Association's office get ransacked.

We drove back down the interstate without incident and I have to say that getting back into our neighborhood was one of the eeriest things I've ever experienced. We were listening to reports on the radio, and it was increasingly clear that all hell had broken loose in the city. It sounded very much like the kind of situation you should be driving *away* from, but there we were driving toward it in the dark. And when we actually reached our neighborhood, darkness was all there was.

We got back just as the light was going—just about that time when streetlights normally start to flicker and storefronts blaze into life. But then, there was nothing: no neon, no warm glow of people's living rooms, no flickering TV light. We were basically driving through streets where there was not even a single traffic light—riding around in complete darkness.

It was as if Katrina had been through there and just sucked all the life out of the place, and replaced it with darkness. That's what it felt like to me, anyway.

Opening the front door, I don't know what I expected, but thankfully, nothing much had changed. So much had changed, of course, but there was no sign of it. I walked on the same carpet, touched the same houseplants. We just didn't have any power or water—that was the only obvious difference. We lit a few candles, dug out some flashlights and thanked God for our good luck.

It was strange that first night, lying there, knowing what was going on just 30 miles away. I say "knowing," but of course we didn't know that much. If I had known what was really going on in the Superdome, maybe it would have been harder to fall asleep.

I later learned that by the time I was safely back in my house, the Superdome had reached a point of overcrowding where the authorities had been obliged to start turning people away. The rescue teams started taking them over to the Ernest N. Morial Convention Center, which had only been slightly damaged in the storm, and so a new nightmare began.

The rescuers were showing up in front of the convention center, where—guess what—there were already a bunch of people waiting. The thing was, the pavement in front of the convention center was dry, and so people had just naturally gravitated there. They were also hoping to get picked up by buses, but that wasn't happening. All this in the heat, remember. Mothers with their babies, with nothing to drink. All they wanted to do was get inside.

But there were already people inside. The convention center's president was in there with a small group of employees manning the fort, as they say. At one point, as darkness was falling, the president came out and told the crowd that there was no food, water or medical care, or any other services of any kind that he could offer them. What happened next was pretty much inevitable. People started breaking in.

By the time I had returned to my house, the crisis at the convention center was just getting going. Because there had never been any plan to admit people there, the situation took a bad turn right from the start.

Crucially, there was no checking for weapons there, as there was at the Superdome. So guns were brought and once a sizeable store of alcohol had been broken into, there was booze. The perfect cocktail. Reports of robberies, assaults, rape and even murder followed.

The next day, a contingent of 250 National Guard soldiers showed up, but not to enforce the law or keep control of the growing crowd; these were engineering units. They just took up residence there, barricaded in for some of the time, watching the people arrive until at one point there was an estimated 20,000.

Then Wednesday came, and waking up, it was incredible how normal everything looked—at least *inside* the house. Outside, it was that same other empty planet.

We kind of groped our way through the day, finding out what was possible and what wasn't. The power came back on, and things seemed even more normal until we had to go to the store for something. Just to go buy milk, we had to drive for over an hour to get into Baton Rouge, where there were still places open. And when the traffic was bad, which it was in those weeks following the storm, it was basically a four-hour round trip.

But of course, this was nothing compared to what was going on in the city.

There, it was just getting worse and worse. By Wednesday, the New Orleans police force was ordered to abandon search and rescue missions and turn their attention to getting a handle on the looting. The city was also put under mandatory curfew. Mayor Nagin called for increased federal assistance, and the same day, Governor Blanco announced the arrival of soldiers, stating that they knew how to shoot and kill and expected to do it.

A Post–Katrina Survival Guide

Despite all this, the craziness and what I can only think to call "mob rule" continued. There were reports of the city descending into total anarchy with widespread looting, carjacking, storm victims being raped and beaten, and fires breaking out. There were bodies everywhere—floating in the water, swelling up in the heat, making it almost impossible for medical examiners to identify the dead.

The crazies were even taking pot shots at the helicopters that were trying to rescue people! The police ended up having to build a temporary jail out of chain link fence in the train station.

At the Superdome, where conditions had continued to deteriorate, people were starting to worry about the floodwater outside, which continued to rise to a depth of three feet. Experts said that if water from Lake Pontchartrain kept flowing, as water tends to do—if it flowed until equilibrium was reached, there would likely be seven feet of water at the Superdome.

I guess the terrible, relentless physics of all this eventually dawned on people, because that very same day, Governor Blanco ordered the whole city, including the Superdome, evacuated.

In fact, a public health emergency was declared for the entire Gulf Coast.

So then, there was this crazy scramble to find places to put people. Relief organizations were struggling to locate suitable facilities to relocate evacuees on a large scale. FEMA announced that it would work with the Greyhound bus company, the Houston Metro and the National Guard to relocate 25,000 people to the Reliant Astrodome in Houston, which was where Barbara Bush made her famous remark about things working out "very well" for all the underprivileged people in there.

By September 1st, which was just three days after the storm, the Astrodome was overflowing and couldn't take any more evacuees. Meanwhile, back at the Superdome in New Orleans, people were still pouring in from the surrounding city. The number of evacuees there was down to 2,500 on that Thursday morning, but by the end of the day, one hour after evacuation had begun, it was filling up again, holding 10,000 more than it had at dawn.

It was as if everything, including the population, had become fluid and was spilling over the barriers we were struggling to put up.

Houston said it would take another 25,000. The George R. Brown Convention Center was opened up. San Antonio also stepped up to the plate, agreeing to house 25,000 more. They made available some vacant office buildings on the grounds of a defunct air force base. The Reunion Arena in Dallas was also opened up to house people. Shelters were set up in Texas, Oklahoma and Arkansas.

Back at the convention center, a contingent of National Guard arrived to establish order and offer the crowd food and water. To deal with all the sick and injured, an emergency triage center was established at the airport. Helicopters and ambulances were bringing in the elderly, the sick, and injured. Airport baggage equipment was used as makeshift gurneys. People were dying of dehydration and exhaustion. Patients requiring ventilators were kept alive with hand-powered resuscitation bags.

By then, buses were taking people from the Superdome...but more kept coming. Fights broke out; there was at least one rape. Dozens were reported to have died, most from heat exhaustion, but the final official death toll inside was six people: four by natural causes, one overdose and one suicide, plus a few more in the flooded area outside the stadium.

Blanco called for 40,000 more National Guard troops to assist in the evacuation of Louisiana, and if necessary, to maintain order. It was around this time that people started to wonder about the availability and readiness of the Louisiana National Guard to do the job they were faced with.

Total Guard strength for the state of Louisiana was 11,000 and at the time Katrina hit, approximately 3,000 of them were serving a tour of duty in Iraq. Basically, one in three of our Guardsmen were missing. It seemed sub-optimal, to say the least.

Of course, both the White House and Pentagon took the position that having a third of their force overseas wasn't going to affect the ability of the Guard to perform their mission. And as it turned out, they were right—at least in terms of the Guard getting the city evacuated.

The whole process was sped up by sending evacuees out to newly opened shelters. The Louis Armstrong International Airport was also reopened to allow flights engaged in relief efforts. The authorities began to put evacuees onto the planes as well.

With all this activity, the Guard and rescue workers began to make an impression on the problem and by Saturday, everyone turned their efforts to the hundreds of people still trapped in area hotels, hospitals, schools and private homes.

Incredibly to me, despite all that was going on, there were still people who would not leave their houses. Apart from everything else, as time went by, there was a serious concern that the flooding was going to cause major health problems for the people trying to cling on. And it wasn't just obvious things like dehydration; there was a risk of hepatitis A infection as well as cholera, tuberculosis and typhoid fever—all diseases that could flourish in the contaminated food and drinking water supplies.

With all the heat, humidity and generalized filth that was swirling around, the city was turning into one giant Petri dish. On September 6th, *E. coli* was detected in the water supply.

Finally, one week after Katrina hit, Mayor Nagin made the decision to order the forced evacuation of everyone from the city who was not involved in the clean up. And still, people clung to their homes.

The eviction efforts were stepped up three days later. Door-to-door searches were conducted to advise remaining residents to leave the city. Finally, National Guard troops had to remove residents by force.

Murder. Mayhem. Anarchy.

My husband saw a lot of it. I thank God I didn't see too much.

Of course, there were tales of heroism, too, like the story of Zeringue Voncelle. She was the property manager at The Esplanade, an apartment building located next to City Park. Zeringue's response to news of the approaching storm was to move her family from her house in Waggaman on the West Bank, to stay at The Esplanade, next to City Park.

Even though she'd been advised by one of the building's co-owners that The Esplanade stood a good chance of being right in Katrina's path, she moved right in there with the intention of toughing it out.

After the levees broke, the lobby of The Esplanade flooded over a foot deep. Zeringue rounded up all the able-bodied residents—there were 170 stranded there, a lot of them seniors, some of them wheelchair-bound, some blind—and named a captain who would be responsible for each floor of the building.

Fortunately for them, there were three cell towers up on the roof, one of which was powered by a generator that worked on natural gas. This meant that they were able to hook up a refrigerator in which to store the residents' supplies of medication and insulin.

They fuelled another generator with gasoline siphoned from cars floating in the parking lot just outside the building. They then used it to charge their cell phones, which enabled them to keep in touch with the owners of the building, except in the immediate aftermath of the storm when service was lost all together.

It was during one of these cell phone conversations with the owners that Zeringue heard a loud explosion, and one of the owners, who was watching coverage on CNN, told her it was gas lines blowing up at a warehouse down at the wharf. After that, her husband turned off the gas and had everyone hand in their candles.

The ordeal was made slightly less traumatic by virtue of the fact that two of the residents, Jerry and Rita Schiffman, owned a restaurant and mini-market store inside the building. They made an effort to cook one decent meal a day, twice cooking out on the rooftop.

While my family and I were settling back into our home, Zeringue and her renters were cooking meals up on the roof, bathing in rainwater and watching the fires that were starting up all over the city. When supplies ran short, there was always the Shell gas station just next door. The military told them to help themselves to whatever they needed.

But things got steadily worse as the days went by. A dead body had become caught between a fence and a tree outside the hotel, and the smell of it rose to the upper floors of the building. Also, there were snakes and rats in the water.

Finally, when the food started to run out, they decided to leave. People came by in a boat and told Zeringue that there was room for three. She picked out a man who was in desperate need of dialysis, a blind man and a man with heart problems. Another boat came by later on and three more elderly people were put on board. But then, they were on their own.

On Thursday, the day after Governor Blanco called for mandatory evacuation of the City of New Orleans , some of The Esplanade's residents waded across the street and stole a boat that was tied up in City Park. They loaded people into the boat and then pulled it into the street, to a bridge where

Zeringue's husband had parked his van. Then, they were able to drive to the New Orleans Museum of Art, where they had seen a helicopter coming in to land.

For the next two days, they ran this makeshift ferry service. One of the residents collapsed and died in the process. Zeringue and her family did this incredible thing until finally the helicopter lifted them to safety, too. The real happy ending came when they got back to their house in Waggaman and found that it had suffered only minimal damage. The electricity came back on the day they returned home.

Stories like that make you almost want things to go wrong sometimes, just to see what people are capable of. Of course, most of what we saw of the aftermath came via the TV, but there were other things that let us know just how close we were to the tragedy—the choppers flying back and forth, for example, and the persistent sound of sirens.

To stop the water flooding through the breaches in the 17th Street, London Avenue and Industrial Canals, helicopters were dropping huge sandbags into the gaps. Later on, they placed barges filled with more sandbags against the ones they'd dropped, hoping to plug up the remaining gaps.

So the choppers were thumping overhead to staunch one flood, and there was this other flood of bedraggled people who just kept pouring out of the city. There were times when it seemed like all the people lucky enough to have a working car had rolled out of the city and were just huddling around Baton Rouge, trying to get over the shock of what had happened.

But apart from the horrendous drives into Baton Rouge, and the general absence of anything you could call creature comforts, we were okay; better than okay, really, and I wanted to get back to work. I wanted to do something, make myself useful to the people I was supposed to represent.

So I started calling around and finally, after a couple of days, I got through to Michele Shane L'Hoste, who is the president of 1st Lake Properties, one of the largest property management companies in the region, representing over 7,000 apartment units.

It was through Michele that I learned that 1st Lake's management and staff were trying to get back to Louisiana. They'd all cleared out and relocated to Texas during the storm and were now looking for hotel rooms.

Laplace was up and running to some degree, but there were absolutely no hotel rooms available; everything was gone. I offered to accommodate some 1st Lake people at my house so that they could be closer to their properties, but they ended up at their property in Baton Rouge.

After a couple of days, word came through that the River Ridge area, where 1st Lake has several apartment communities, had suffered minimal damage and—what was more significant, in a way—no flooding. So they decided to try to set up a center of operations there.

The plan was simple: basically, set up shop and get apartments back on line to house all the folks who were in desperate need of shelter. To me, it seemed like a good idea, so since I was just sitting there twiddling my thumbs, I offered my services to 1st Lake. Like I said, I wanted to get back into the thick of it and help out if I could—at least until we figured out what was going to happen with the Apartment Association.

Michele welcomed me aboard. She told me to get over to River Ridge as soon as possible. She said there was work to be done.

That turned out to be one of the biggest understatements of all time.

CHAPTER THREE

Chaos

Hickory Creek is an apartment community located outside Metairie, between Lake Pontchartrain and the Mississippi River, in a place called River Ridge. Pre–Katrina, it was a pleasant development in landscaped grounds, but it took a battering during the storm; just how much of a battering, I found out on the morning of September 7th.

Getting there from Laplace was usually a 20 to 25 minute drive but that morning, there were police and National Guard soldiers just everywhere—manning roadblocks, controlling the flow of traffic, slowing things down. To get into River Ridge (and it was the same getting into any parish outside of Saint John, certainly anything going toward New Orleans), I had to have a pass and I had to show my driver's license, which is what I did.

And then I was through.

Hickory Creek is one of 1st Lake Properties' biggest complexes, with over 450 units. I say 'units' because that's just the language we use, but another way to say it is "homes." And that was what I was looking at when I finally arrived: 450 homes with all the bedding, carpet, furniture, TVs, pictures, gizmos, toasters and refrigerators that you would expect to find.

I walked through about 150 homes on that first day, often with a hand over my nose and mouth because of the stench, taking stock, opening doors, shaking my head. Okay, the units weren't gutted, but they were damaged. There were even some that were roof-damaged, which had led to considerable flooding.

And hovering in the background, as I made my inventory, were the people; people just desperate to get back into their homes, or people who'd come from elsewhere and were trying to get a roof over their heads.

On the other side of that equation were the owners—just as devastated, in a different way. They were standing around open-mouthed, looking at their building in disbelief, wondering where their tenants had gone.

They had scattered everywhere. Katrina refugees fled in droves—upwards of 35,000 into Texas and 24,000 into Mobile, Alabama, alone; Baton Rouge absorbed 15,000, and it was like that all across the south. People went to Houston, Dallas, Fort Worth, Austin, San Antonio…

Of course, one of the reasons for the exodus was the great work done by Apartment Associations in finding them places to go. Pretty much immediately after the storm hit, the National Apartment Association got its membership mobilized to help the half million people the storm had left homeless, and sympathetic apartment owners from around the country started calling in, offering help or putting listings up on the HurricaneHousing.net website.

A Post–Katrina Survival Guide

That's one of the things about disasters—maybe the one silver lining: they bring out the good in people. Even if the media all too often wanted to focus on stories of price gouging and looting, there were plenty of stories of generosity. There was the Camden Property Trust in Houston, the closest metropolitan area to New Orleans, which offered 30 fully furnished units rent-free for two months so that people would have places to stay while they got back on their feet.

Or Strong Management in Winter Park, Florida, which owns a total of 1,400 units. Strong donated nine apartments in its bigger communities, with a free seven-month lease and free utilities. The company also provided furniture, housewares and even clothing.

And there were examples like that in Dallas, in Birmingham, in Memphis... In fact, I was often amazed at how much the owners and management companies were ready to do to help, whether it was allowing people who were transferring to another state to get out of their leases with deposits refunded in full, or agreeing to remove flood damaged furniture at no charge, or actually finding them places to stay. I was just very proud of what our members found it in themselves to do.

Unfortunately, generosity wasn't enough.

Because there was a real problem there. Even at Hickory Creek, which, as I said before, wasn't that badly damaged by the storm. People didn't see it at first; they couldn't see beyond the obvious physical damage that had been done to the building, to the logistical nightmare that was looming. In fact, as the days went by, it became more and more clear that nobody really had any idea how to deal with the situation.

On the face of it, the problem was pretty simple. You had on the one hand these units that were uninhabitable, water-damaged, reeking of mold and rotting food; and on the other, these people—homeless people, which included first responders and work crews who had come in to sort out the mess.

The logical thing to do was fix up the units, even if only on a temporary basis, and get the people inside. And in fact, that was where the work crews started—trying to bring the building back on line. But immediately, they ran into legal issues.

The problem was, the rotting, waterlogged sofa sitting in the middle of that living room, which looked like it might be about to go through the rotting floor, belonged to somebody. You couldn't just drag it out and throw it away, even if it was about to cause tens of thousands of dollars' worth of damage. You just couldn't do it. No, you had to find the renters and get them to sign a waiver saying you could yank the couch.

So that's what the owners started trying to do. They called off the work crews and struggled to get in touch with the renters, and then if they were lucky enough to find them, got them to sign a waiver. They were generating all kinds of improvised paperwork, getting it signed, then having the crews drag the waterlogged stuff out, partly to clear the way for repair and partly to prevent further degradation to the floors, the walls, the ceilings…

And if they couldn't find the tenants, they just moved on to the next unit and started the process again.

And you have to remember, this was all happening in tremendous heat and humidity, and happening all over the city, in many places on a much bigger scale. In Lakeview, for example, only a couple of miles away, there was a pile of trash from gutted properties stacked three stories high on West End Boulevard. Crews were throwing up from the smell, going in and out of the properties wearing respirators.

There were times when I thought I'd throw up myself. It wasn't just the stink of moldy carpets and furniture, although that was bad enough. One of the biggest challenges in the apartment complexes that hadn't been affected by the flooding or suffered a lot of storm damage was the refrigerators.

People had cleared out, leaving them packed with food—raw chicken, leftovers, milk cartons, you name it. Every property management company that I spoke to was having refrigerators replaced left and right, because they were just full of maggots and the smell…that smell…it was enough to knock you down.

So, as I said, waivers were being signed and properties were getting cleared, but then the moment arrived when the owners had to deal with the problem that came to plague us in the weeks to come: the absent tenants. These people were just nowhere around. They'd either left, leaving no contact information whatsoever, or had left contact information that was inaccurate or out of date.

At that point, the owners had no choice but to start evictions on the grounds of abandonment, which is exactly what they did. In the end, it was the only legal way to carry on with the repairs.

So a rough *modus operandi* was established: evict on abandonment, clear out the unit, then rip out the carpets, the dry wall (or in this case wet wall) and whatever else had been ruined by the water. And this was how it went on for those first few days.

As soon as they were able, 1st Lake Properties set up a command post at Citrus Creek Apartments, which was no more than half a mile away. They were having a tremendous struggle just trying to get all their staff back. Once they'd gotten them back, they were faced with the challenge of finding them somewhere to stay.

Remember, they were having to house employees who had lost everything. They were housing contractors, they were housing work crews. Guys were sleeping in trailers on Bullard Avenue. City Park became a kind of Hooverville, with tents and trailers set up under the cypress trees. There were even cruise ships chartered to try to accommodate people.

Because there were no restaurants or diners or eateries of any kind open in Metairie, the 1st Lake people were also having to truck in food and water and other supplies from Baton Rouge. They were feeding their employees and contractors 3 meals a day, and these guys were hungry after ripping up wet apartments for 12 hours at a stretch, believe me.

For a couple of weeks, 1st Lake struggled on in these difficult conditions as all around them something like normalcy began to return to the Metairie/Jefferson Parish area.

By that time, the board members of the Apartment Association of New Orleans were starting to get back in touch, and the question everyone was asking was, "What are we going to do with the Apartment Association?"

Now, these weren't always the calmest of conversations. People were under a lot of stress. Like 1st Lake, they all had their own individual situations to deal with at their own properties.

This is something people tend to forget, of course: that the owners themselves were struggling, and not just with their housing stock or their tenants. Katrina hit them where they worked—just as she had hit the Apartment Association of Greater New Orleans. She put out their lights just as she put out ours.

HRI Properties, for example, a full-service real estate development company located on Baronne Street in the heart of the business district, took the full brunt of the storm and had to scramble for its survival in the aftermath. In many ways, HRI's experience in the months following Katrina is emblematic of what many companies went through.

HRI also helped us in the preparation of the hurricane preparedness guide, which we distributed to all our owners this year, and their contribution was priceless because they saw the devastation of Katrina up close, and dealt with it remarkably well.

A Post–Katrina Survival Guide

HRI has 12 affordable and market-rate apartment and condominium communities, as well as three hotels in New Orleans. They were all affected by Katrina, suffering deterioration that ranged from minor roof damage and leaks to flooding, and wind and water damage. They also were also the target of looters.

As for HRI's staff, they were scattered all over the state and some of them even lost their homes. They showed tremendous dedication in working to get the company back on its feet—many people actually left their families to do so.

HRI was fortunate—or I suppose you could say smart—to have all records of their operations protected by backup servers and Web-based databases, but they were still caught unaware, just like the rest of us. Its 70 or so employees left work on Friday the 26th just like we at the Association did, assuming that Katrina was headed for Florida.

Because of that, they never got to communicate with their staff or their residents. Computers and cell phones were highly unreliable in the aftermath of the storm, and telephone service in the 504 area code, which covers New Orleans, was down. In the first hours and days, text messaging was the best they could do to be in touch.

So HRI's staff had no simple way of finding out if their company had shut down, or for how long, or whether there was any likelihood of their getting paid. As for their residents, they didn't know how long they were going to be put out of their apartments, or where they needed to go if they wanted to report damage to their units. Basically, everyone was cut off from each other.

As a result of that experience, HRI now makes sure it has not only every employee's cell phone number, it also asks for e-mail addresses and emergency contact phone numbers outside the local area code.

Despite the prevailing chaos, the Tuesday after Katrina hit—*i.e.*, the very next day—a small group of HRI executives and managers gained entry to the Baronne Street headquarters and started the laborious task of recovering essential records and computer hardware. They also checked for damage to the building, including signs of looting.

This meant entering a darkened building and walking up and down 17 floors carrying box files and computers. As it turned out, their prompt response and considerable effort paid off because where there were plenty of owners who lost everything in the hurricane, none of HRI's crucial architectural drawings had been damaged. And it was the same for their servers, terminals and laptop computers.

Once they recovered their records and hardware, they were faced with the task of setting up satellite operations in locations as close to headquarters as they could manage. Again, they got lucky there, becoming aware of an opportunity through staff contacts.

By Wednesday, they were looking at a 10,000 square-foot office space in Houma, Louisiana, which was within an hour's drive of the Baronne Street headquarters. But lucky or not, they still had to move fast—since another would-be tenant was right there, virtually waving a wad of cash. This meant that HRI had limited scope for negotiation and had to make a very big decision very quickly, which is what they did.

And maybe fortune does favor the brave, because not only did they get the 10,000 square feet of office space, they also found apartments nearby to house staff. As it turned out, the sister of one of the company's New Orleans' property managers ran an apartment community next to the temporary office in Houma.

Staff members were obliged to bunk up in these units and were in some cases separated from their families, but they did it to keep HRI running. Three months later, they vacated the Houma space and continued to pay rent on it, but no one at the company regrets the decision because it kept HRI up and running at a very difficult time.

With owners going through this kind of trauma and struggle, you can imagine that what to do with the Apartment Association wasn't exactly at the top of their "to-do" lists. We were asking them to forget about their own problems and focus on the broader needs of the Apartment Association community, and these needs were enormous.

At one level, the city, the owners and their tenants had never needed us more, but things were so crazy, it was hard to define exactly what needs we could hope to meet. There was some talk about making the Association a part-time thing, which apart from anything else would have meant my looking for another job to supplement my income.

In the end, we called an emergency board meeting and came to the view that with everything that was going on, the Association should stay open full-time. We'd work out what we could do as we went along and in the meantime, we would at least be there for our owners.

At this point, we didn't even have an office—not one you could sit in and get anything done in, anyway. Compared to a lot of other places in the city, we'd gotten off pretty light, but there was still some damage. We had broken windows and water was coming in. But miracle of miracles, we had somehow avoided getting looted!

But looted or not, there was no way I was going to sit in a puddle of water and make phone calls. So I decided to take everything out of the Association office and open up shop at my house. In fact, I was up and running from my home as soon as I could get into the city, which was around September 5th.

I had the telephone company transfer the Association's number to my house so that when people called, they'd have someone to speak to. After that, I was rolling, and beginning to feel a real sense of purpose. We weren't just going to be reacting to circumstances—we were going to come up with a plan to get units back on line and get tenants back into homes.

We were just getting ready to start making a difference when something terrible happened. It wasn't an act of God this time. But it did come from on high.

CHAPTER FOUR

Acts of God and Acts of Governors

One week into the clean up, around September 14th, an executive order came down from Governor Kathleen Blanco's office to the effect that no one in the state of Louisiana could evict anyone for any reason. The order had in fact been issued on September 6th but with the general lack of communication, it took a while for it to get to us.

No Evictions. Of anyone. For any reason. It has a ring to it, doesn't it? You can just hear the wheels of the judicial system grinding to a halt. Which is of course exactly what they did.

Blanco's decision was radical, but then so was the situation we were faced with, and it was like everything else we were doing at the time: *ad hoc*, impromptu, made up. We didn't really have a plan, not as a city, not as a nation, not as a society. And when you don't have a plan, "solutions"—the fixes you come up with to deal with acute and immediate problems—can rapidly become part of a whole set of fresh new problems that then require some even newer solutions and so on into the eye of the storm…

At first glance, to some people anyway, Blanco's move made some kind of cockeyed sense. The city was in turmoil, the courts were in turmoil and what she was trying to do was put all the pending malpractice and civil cases—including eviction proceedings—on hold while everything was so out of whack.

There was also some concern about price-gouging by the few bad apple landlords who had warmed to the notion that canceling old leases and replacing them with higher-paying new leases might be a pretty good way of making some extra cash. So let's say that Kathleen Blanco meant well—but she stirred up a storm of her own.

For one thing, as I believe already mentioned, the only chance the owners had of rescuing their buildings was to get all the sopping wet furniture, carpet and sheet rock out. And if they couldn't evict the absent tenant, then they certainly couldn't touch their stuff.

Moreover, getting that stuff out wasn't at that point just a question of staring-you-in-the-face common sense; the insurance companies had started demanding that the owners "mitigate" damage in the aftermath of the storm on the understanding that failure to do so could result in problems with coverage. Now, you know how picky insurance assessors can be—so you also know my owners were taking those mitigation instructions seriously.

We sucked it up for a week or so, struggling with the day-to-day, worrying about yet another storm out there in the Gulf heading our way.

What?

Yes, it was kind of hard to get our heads round. Another one? After all we'd been through? She went by the name of Rita that time, but Rita, Rhonda or Renée, she was doing more or less the same dance Katrina did, sucking up heat in the Gulf and spinning her way in our direction.

Understandably storm-shy by this time, Mayor Nagin, who had been planning on officially reopening the city on September 19th, cancelled those plans and initiated a re-evacuation of the city on September 21st. Of course, once people started moving out again, it started to feel like we really were in for it a second time, and everyone was saying, "She's coming straight for us, she's coming straight for us."

But in the end, she wasn't. Rita more or less passed us by. I say "more or less" because although she remained well to the south and west of New Orleans, she did manage to push out what the weather people called a "pre-landfall storm surge" and what I'd call a big wave that had enough zing in it to breach a levee that was supposedly protecting the Lower 9th Ward.

The water strained part of the levee system that was already weakened by Katrina and once again, parts of New Orleans, the 9th Ward mainly, were under water. So we sat Rita out, then kept working on the building as best we could. But with the executive order hanging over us, it was pretty much impossible.

So on September 28th, on behalf of the Apartment Association of Greater New Orleans, I drew myself up to my full height and wrote Blanco a letter, asking her to reconsider her order. And just so that we at the Association wouldn't be misunderstood, we spelled it all out as plain as plain. One, there were missing tenants who could not be reached. Two, the stuff belonging to those missing people was falling to bits because of moisture and mold. Three, the units containing those belonging were deteriorating as a result.

I asked Governor Blanco to work with the multi-family housing industry to come up with a reasonable solution for owners to regain possession of their units.

And do you know what she wrote back?

Nothing.

And yes, I think she got my letter. For some reason it just didn't merit a reply. Maybe set against all the suffering that was going on, the financial discomfort of a few thousand owners didn't amount to much. I'm just speculating, of course...Or maybe she, or her staff, were just too busy.

But then a couple of interesting little dynamics started up—little eddies in the storm Blanco had initiated. One had to do with the "you can't evict for any reason" side of her order. Somehow, certain people got it into their pointy little heads that since they couldn't be thrown out into the street anymore, it might be an idea just to stop paying rent.

That's right, because—surprise, surprise—some of the more enterprising people in Baton Rouge, or Lafayette, or Lake Charles and on up to Shreveport, enterprising people living in properties that had sustained no damage whatsoever during the storm suddenly found that they lacked a compelling reason to write that monthly check. There were people literally calling up owners and saying, "I'm not paying my rent because you can't evict me!"

And then there was the second dynamic—a more serious one, because it had to do with all the homeless people. You know, the victims of the storm? Because it turned out that when you looked at it real close, the owners' problem (the one that Blanco didn't think was worth addressing) was also *their* problem.

Insofar as they wanted to move into the units the owners wanted to clean up, they shared the same problem as the owners. The owners would have liked to rent to them and *would* have rented to them, if they'd been able to evict the TENANTS WHO WERE NO LONGER AROUND.

Suzanne Rouse, a manager with Tonti Management, a Metairie property management firm, put it well when she told a local paper that "government officials continue to report on the housing shortage while failing to acknowledge the hundreds and hundreds of apartments that stand vacant or in need of repairs yet remain inaccessible to landlords due to the governor's order."

And she wasn't alone in feeling that way. Henry Shane, one of the owners of 1st Lake Properties, a member of the Apartment Association and chairman of Favrot & Shane, which has about 8,000 units mainly on the east bank of Jefferson Parish, said he had 1,800 abandoned units that he would have liked to free up through the eviction process. Extrapolating his case for the whole city, he figured that of the 50,000 units in complexes of 100-plus units, there were probably between 20,000 to 30,000 in the same predicament.

Like I did, Henry wrote to Blanco, asking her to give him control of his property. And it wasn't just a question of making units available; he wanted to protect the welfare of the residents in the undamaged units who were living alongside all the moldering junk. Because that was another aspect of it: rotting couches filled with vermin were a health hazard!

Like me, he got no reply.

We needed some leverage. We needed some heft. We needed some muscle.

We called the National Apartment Association. We called the National Apartment Association's legal counsel. We invited them all to New Orleans to ask for their participation and support in writing another letter to the Governor; preferably a letter she'd feel like answering.

And it occurred to us, since we were going to have all these good people in New Orleans, why not give them the tour?

They arrived in the first week of October, a group that included President Tom Day, whose firm Hepfner, Smith, Airhart & Day runs apartment communities in New Orleans; Executive VP Doug Culkin, NAA legal counsel John McDermott, State and Local Policy Manager Freeman Smith and a PR consultant by the name of Stacey Kerans.

We started out with a private meeting in which we tried to explain the various social, physical and legal challenges we faced. Then we moved onto a press event where property owners were given free rein to talk about what they were going through.

It went pretty well. Some local television people showed up as well as reporters from NBC Nightly News and the local New Orleans paper, *The Times-Picayune*. It felt like we were really getting the word out there about how harmful Blanco's ban was.

After that was over, we took the NAA people on a little tour.

We picked out three apartment communities, figuring that would be enough to make the point. The worst of them was a place called Wind Run. It was managed by Volunteers of America and located in East New Orleans, part of the city that was particularly badly affected by the storm.

We rolled through the neighborhoods, pointing out all the blue tarps on the roofs. The Army Corps of Engineers had installed them as part of Operation Blue Roof, an attempt to protect homes from further inundations. By the end of October, there were over 50,000 tarps in place like blue Band-aids on the victim of a train wreck.

We reached the apartment building and parked next to some abandoned cars that were caked with mud. There were cars everywhere, trash everywhere. The entry gate looked like it had been hit by a tank. All the way around the building, there was this line, like a ring left by dirty bathwater that had climbed to about five feet off the ground. Inside, it was worse, of course.

Like every other flood-damaged building I'd been inside over the past two months, it stank. The carpet squelched underfoot. There was mold all over the walls and the cabinets. But it was seeing folks' personal possessions that always got to me. I walked into units on the ground floors of these buildings and it looked like someone had taken everything you can imagine as being part of someone's life—clothing, pictures, photographs of children and grandchildren—and they'd put it all inside a snow globe and then shaken it hard. Really hard.

I remember walking into one unit and seeing this child's bedroom. There was a brand new baby bed, and inside the baby's closet, there were all these clothes—brand new, still with the tags from the store. It had to be someone who had just had a child or was expecting a child and they'd had to just up and leave everything behind.

As you can imagine, all that was fairly depressing. We walked around the Wind Run apartment building for a while and then drove around the city, taking in the Convention Center. Ironically enough, that was where the NAA Education Conference was supposed to be held in June of the following year.

We looked at the Cruise Ships that still housed evacuees and relief workers. We took a good look at all this, and these folks who had come from all over the country looked at us and said, "We've seen the pictures, and we've heard the news, but until you come here, until you see it, touch it and smell it, you have no way of knowing what it really is—what a disaster this really is and what ordinary working Americans are going through."

Ordinary Americans. Us. It made me think.

The tour helped. It helped that they saw and smelled and understood. It galvanized them. But by that time—maybe because of all the media attention, or maybe because she just saw the light—Kathleen Blanco had lifted her ban. The NAA people first got wind of it that day, when we showed them the town. Doug Culkin got a call from a journalist on his cell.

As soon as the executive order was lifted, which was on October 25th—except in the Lake Charles area, which had been hit by hurricane Rita; the ban wasn't lifted there until November 25th—owners began filing eviction requests. Thousands of them.

The process took about 10 days to work through the system, and then the local constables were dispatched, going from property to property serving the notices, which, in the absence of tenants, they did by putting them on the doors.

Naturally enough, there was concern among certain members of the community that the lifting of the ban would result in unjust evictions and people who had already suffered being brutally turned into the street. And there were probably some instances of that kind of thing.

But there was plenty of frustration and anxiety among owners, too; owners who had been kept waiting around for months watching their property deteriorate and their capital bleed away. For people like Henry Shane, the damage could be calculated in millions of dollars, but smaller owners suffered as well. In fact, in many ways they suffered more because they didn't have the cash flow to keep them afloat or the backing of friendly banks.

There was a real risk of going under for people like Janet Soto, an independent owner with just 20 apartments on her books. She struggled to make her monthly mortgage payments in the absence of tenants and once the ban was finally lifted, she went around with her 16-year-old boy, clearing damaged units of mildewed furniture with her own hands.

Meanwhile, the constables went about their work, knocking on doors, sticking up notices, moving on. The work crews went in behind them and started dragging stuff out. It piled up in the streets, where it was picked over by others in what came to resemble some sort of grotesque, giant yard sale. It was all pretty grim, but there was a sense of progress being made.

This went on for about a month, and then another ruling came down from on high—from the Federal Court this time, and the gavel of Judge Stanwood Duval.

As of November 22nd, all pending evictions were put on hold until landlords sent eviction notices directly to their tenants. Any eviction hearing could not take place until 45 days after those mailings were postmarked.

"No longer can landlords just rely on tacking notices on doors while the tenants don't know they're getting evicted," said Judith Browne, lead attorney for the plaintiffs. "It's going to provide fair rules so that people can come and defend themselves and, ultimately, protect their property."

The settlement was the outcome of a lawsuit brought November 10th by unions, activists and individual renters, against every parish and city official who dealt with evictions in Orleans and Jefferson. And while it wasn't too difficult to see their point of view—after all, a tenant might be elsewhere, in Houston with family, for example, and might not be in a position to look at his or her door—the ruling did once again put all the burden of sorting out the mess we were in back onto the shoulders of the owners.

The Federal Emergency Management Agency (FEMA) did offer some help to the owners by committing to supplying court clerks, constables and justices of the peace with the addresses of evacuees upon request, but there was an expectation that owners would be able to provide some addresses. Back at the Association, we knew it was still going to be an uphill struggle tracking those people down.

So the clock was once again ticking for the likes of Henry Shane and Janet Soto. As Bill Quigley, one of the representatives for the plaintiffs, put it at the time, "There won't be any eviction hearings next week or the week after, or for at least 45 days."

Of course, the whole thing from our perspective was a complete mess. It pretty much took us back to square one, into which we'd first been dropped by Governor Blanco. At best, it was going to take months for owners to get an eviction.

So once again, we at the Association rolled up our sleeves, and in partnership with New Orleans Metro Board of Realtors and the Home Builders Multi Family Apartment Counsel Division, we hired a local lawyer and got in touch with National Apartment Association legal counsel John McDermott to ask him to intervene. Letters were written, letters were mailed.

As of March 1, 2006, Judge Duval's ruling was lifted from most areas but remained in place for certain parts of the east bank of Orleans Parish. We kept on slugging and the case was finally heard in June, when the judge decided to go ahead and lift the ruling completely.

Looking back at that morning when I walked into the Hickory Creek apartment community, I realize how naïve I was about the challenge we at the Association faced. We thought it was about the buildings and the people. But it was about a whole lot more than that.

Mainly it was about what happens when society doesn't have a real plan (by which I mean an administrative, judicial, logistical, financial and above all social plan) in place to deal with disaster on that staggering a scale.

When you're faced with a city that is under a couple of feet of filthy water, you think you're looking at an engineering problem. Get the water out, get the buildings dry, get the people back in. That's as near as you get to conceiving a plan. It has taken me 12 months to understand, but that isn't even the half of it.

CHAPTER FIVE

Supply and Demand

Choke off the supply of any commodity and you're going to see a jump in prices. It's a simple truth of the marketplace but of course, in the case of New Orleans—in the case of post-Katrina New Orleans—there are no simple truths.

We're not talking about demand for plasma screen TVs, after all. We're talking about people standing in line like they did outside the brand new apartment building in Gonzalez, a town outside Baton Rouge. That building was completed just after Katrina swept through, and people stood in line from before dawn to try to get into decent accommodation; people were desperate enough to fight for their places in line. That's how it was in Gonzalez, where every unit was signed up on the first day.

Real Estate Disasters

Even without Governor Blanco's and Judge Duval's interventions, the property available to the people of New Orleans was drastically reduced in the months following the hurricane. Katrina destroyed something like 122,000 owner-occupied homes and wiped another 84,000 rental properties off the market. Meanwhile, people were on the move, pouring into areas like Baton Rouge, which saw an influx of over 100,000 in those first weeks.

And again, it's one thing to talk about the numbers, but to be in the middle of it, to see the traffic, to be stuck in traffic, to have to stand in line at a Walgreens for two hours as I had to in order to get a prescription filled—that brings a different order of understanding.

There's a grinding misery to a broken city that the statistics don't show, and if you add to that all the uncertainty, the fear of ending up in the street that a lot of Katrina victims had to cope with, well I think it's only then that you start to imagine how it was.

Of course, not everyone was doing so badly. Some local realtors, for example, were making out just fine. One of the side effects of the housing shortage was the creation of a hot little market in certain kinds of real estate. Among the big buyers post-Katrina were corporations looking for properties, with views to securing housing for their employees.

This sounds kind of altruistic, and maybe at some level it was, but basically, the companies were in the same predicament as 1st Lake Properties: their staff had been scattered to the four winds.

One of the things I remember from the time just after storm—it's a memory as vivid as blue tarps on the rooftops or the mud-caked cars strewn all over the city—was the signs posted on neutral ground, advertising for workers. Everywhere you looked, it was, "Workers needed, workers needed." Fast food outlets were giving out $500 signing bonuses just to get people in to work for them.

One of the results of this was to draw new workers in from outside, something that radically changed the racial make up of the city. Pre-Katrina, the population of New Orleans was predominantly African American, but the influx of Latino workers, many of them migrant workers, changed all that. These were people who were ready to work hard all day and then go home to a tent in City Park where they'd spend the night.

For some people, this influx of outsiders was seen as a sinister attempt by local government to dilute the African American character of the city. It was the same sort of conspiracy thinking that claimed the levees were breached deliberately, the same sort of thinking that gave rise to one of the of the sadder jokes going around at the time—that FEMA stood for "Find Every Mexican Available."

But the reality of it was that the corporations needed staff. While not having enough people is a major headache for a company the size of 1st Lake, for a corporation the size of a Wal-Mart or a Shell or a Chevron, it's a humongous, blinding migraine.

I got a sense of the pain of it when I was at the Hickory Creek apartment complex. People from these corporations, and I'm talking about presidents and CEOs sometimes, were coming in ready to pay top dollar to see their employees housed, coming in every single day. And, of course, they didn't want just one or two units; they wanted 10 or 15. And you'd better believe they had money to spend.

But the money didn't make any difference. By that time, the market was just too hot. CEO or not, you're still acting on the information available and by the time you read the ad on the Website or got the call from the realtor, the property was gone.

Real Estate Disasters

Scarcity of decent properties pushed up the rental rates all over the city by something like seven to 10 percent in the aftermath of the storm, but in certain pockets, they got much higher. What this meant was that at a certain point, these corporations were looking at properties that cost $4,000 a month to rent, but only $2,500 to finance through a home loan. And once the scales tipped that way, the corporations started buying.

Shell was one of the first. They started snapping up single-family homes, condominiums, travel trailers, even apartment complexes. And needless to say, there were plenty of realtors around ready to help them meet their needs.

In Laplace, my neck of the woods, you could see the realtors going door to door, looking for homeowners who might be ready to sell. And I guess they must have found some because Shell's holdings of residential real estate went from zero pre-Katrina to a portfolio of 130 properties within just a few weeks of the storm; a portfolio of properties worth in the region of $32 million.

Most of what they bought was within driving distance of their company operations—places like Tangipahoa, St. John the Baptist, Ascension, St. Tammany, Livingston and East and West Baton Rouge. All of those areas were within striking distance of their training facility in Robert.

As it turned out, they never even used the apartment complexes they bought in Hammond, one of which had 44 units and the other 52. But having come out ahead on every deal where they've decided to sell, I don't think they're too worried about holding onto them.

Chevron had the same problem as Shell but took a different route to solve it—they purchased some 60 trailers and leasing property in Carencro and Picayune, Mississippi. I hear they still own the trailers even though the employees have all moved out. The word is, they're hanging onto them for the time being, waiting to see what happens this hurricane season.

Associated Terminals, which is a local stevedoring company that runs the Chalmette slip for the Port of St. Bernard, had about 90 employees living in the parish at the time of the storm. It moved them to a housing vessel that the company was actually working on and then parked more trailers on another ship. They also purchased 19 houses in Laplace, Reserve and Wallace to accommodate some St. Bernard workers who were shifted to the Associated Terminal operations in Reserve.

With hurricane Katrina, Kathleen Blanco and Stanwood Duval removing whole swaths of property from the market, and the likes of Shell snapping up all the good, dry, solid, conveniently located stuff, there was only one way for prices to go, and that was up. This isn't to criticize the corporations—in fact Shell, for example, has tried to do its bit for the city in the past year, selling properties to the employees living in them in some cases and even renting to employees at pre-Katrina rates in others.

But the overall effect of their throwing their money around was undoubtedly to put tremendous pressure on prices. College students returning to the city for the start of classes were faced with rent increases that could be as high as 40 percent. A lot of them were finding that the only way they could afford to keep roofs over their heads was to double up on joint leases.

Meanwhile, the rents in downtown New Orleans and the Warehouse District, which were always the highest in the city at around $1.25 to $1.35 per square foot pre-Katrina, were pushing up to $1.60 per square foot and looked like they were headed for $2 per by the year's end. The prices were driven by landlords' having to defray the costs of their new insurance contracts; companies like HRI Management saw the insurance on its 228-unit condominium called the Cotton Mill climb 80 percent in January.

While the cost and scarcity of accommodation was mainly a problem for people trying to rent, the cost of rebuilding was a problem that hit my owners directly. And it wasn't the only problem they faced. A lack of building materials, the glacially slow pace of insurance settlements and an increasingly acute labor shortage were just some of the issues preventing owners from getting on with rehabilitating their rental stock.

Take Favrot & Shane, for example, a company with about 8,000 apartment units in the metropolitan area. Of their 2,300 units damaged by Hurricane Katrina, five months after the storm, only 500 had been brought back on line. Through February and March, the company was bringing units back at the rate of 100 per month, all of which were already spoken for; such was the demand at that time.

Rehabilitation was haphazard. There were pockets of activity next to pockets of decay. Just from the point of view of purchasing materials, owners were suddenly facing a very steep hill. Lumber, nails, piping, dry wall—everything went up in price post-Katrina. And of course, to rebuild, you needed workers and for there to be workers, there needed to be homes…and so it went on. Sometimes, it seemed to me that the city was like a dog chasing its own tail.

You could drive a down a street in Metairie and see crews working frantically to get a building finished by sundown while on the opposite sidewalk, another building stood completely abandoned, just as it had been the day after the storm. More often than not, the empty buildings belonged to owners waiting for insurance settlements.

Owners with companies big enough to fund repairs out of their own capital got on with it. People like Mtumishi St. Julien of the nonprofit New Orleans Housing Authority, whose 263-unit Willows complex suffered flooding as deep as four feet on the first floor, had almost finished rehabilitation by the end of January. Gene Ratchford, a property developer and manager out of North Carolina got to work on his 216-unit Pepper Cove apartment complex in east New Orleans straight away. He took the settlement offered by his insurer and went to work, looking to be open for business by July.

Similarly, Ken Heller and his partner Howard Stone of Pride Property of Denver went ahead and renovated 150 units of their 444-unit Esplanade at City Park, and started moving pre-Katrina tenants back in. Heller and Stone's story is as a shining example of how storm insurance and recovery should work. They began ordering equipment, working in coordination with HRH Insurance of Savannah, Georgia, on August 28th, and 10 days later, they were holding the settlement checks in their hands.

That's how it was supposed to work, but generally speaking, it did not. For every example of things going smoothly, there were 10 more of things screwing up, of owners getting tangled in red tape or finding that the coverage they thought had, they didn't.

On top of everything else, our owners were faced with a huge bump in insurance rates. This was true for anyone along the Gulf Coast and was particularly true for wind coverage, the cost of which just skyrocketed.

The case of HRI, a New Orleans apartment and housing developer, is pretty typical. As related above, the company came out of the hurricane more or less intact but with a lot of repairs to carry out. So, management set about the work, knowing that it was covered by its insurance policy.

In May, HRI's policy expired and management was told that their premium was going to jump 400 percent. Instead of paying out $500,000 every year, the company would then have to pay $2.5 million. On top of that, HRI was told that its deductible for wind damage was also going to rise from one to five percent. On a wind damage claim for a $10 million property, the deductible would then be a hefty $500,000.

Real Estate Disasters

To add insult to injury, the insurers let HRI know that it was going to have to lower the maximum payout for any given claim from $200 million to $50 million.

This was a scenario played out all over the city and the effect was twofold: on the one hand it made it very unattractive for property development or management companies to come in from the outside and do business there; on the other, it forced the companies already committed into somehow absorbing the new costs.

The big worry was that companies in that position would have to raise their rents, which is exactly what HRI did after the storm. For their existing tenants they put up the rent 10 or even 20 percent at renewal time, and for the new clients they raised 25 percent. The other option open to owners was to cut overhead by reducing maintenance staff and cutting corners on repairs and upkeep.

To stop insurance companies from dropping their clients after the storm, the Louisiana Department of Insurance introduced what was known as Rule 23, which basically made it impossible for an insurer to do that, at least until December 31st. But it made no provision for keeping down premiums. As a last resort, owners were able to go to the Louisiana Citizens Property Insurance Corporation, but their rates were higher than those available on the open market.

When HRI's insurers started offering reduced coverage at a higher rate, they invoked Rule 23 and took their insurers to court, where the judge forced the RSUI Group, Inc. of Atlanta to continue to provide the same coverage at the same rate.

These were the kinds of battles being fought on a daily basis by our owners, who were struggling to survive. Luckily for us at the Association, our owners were pretty much all we had to worry about. Someone else was trying to carry the whole city, and that someone was FEMA.

They had come into the devastated city in the days following the storm in their emergency management role, and were then—I'm talking about late October, early November—trying to get a handle on the recovery process.

They reached out for local help, talking to local authorities and anyone who could offer useful input on what were complex issues. So, getting together with Greater New Orleans, Incorporated, a regional economic alliance, we at the Association put together a Housing Task Force which consisted of us, New Orleans realtors, the Home Builders Association and banking finance and investment groups. We didn't have FEMA's money or resources, but we did have an understanding of the rental market in our city, and we were more than ready to share it.

Of course, by that time, FEMA was heavily committed to certain aspects of their strategy. One of those aspects was the decision, made within days of the disaster, to buy temporary homes to provide accommodation for the victims of the storm. In fact, just under $3 billion of the $7.15 billion they'd committed to housing displaced families at that time had gone into trailers and mobile homes.

And we're not just talking about buying boxes with wheels on them here; we're talking about setting up entire trailer parks, which of course meant renting land and then putting in all the necessary water, sewage and other utilities to make the park viable. Most of the land they leased was in sparsely populated suburbs, or what the town planners call "exurbs" and I call the middle of nowhere around Louisiana and Mississippi.

It was a decision that came back to haunt them.

Right from the start, it was clear that the trailers were not the most efficient allocation of resources. Despite representing—in dollar terms—something like 40 percent of what was initially allocated for displaced families, only 125,000 of the estimated

600,000 families without homes had moved into those so-called communities at that time.

And what's more, because of logistical problems or, in some cases, resistance by local communities to having the trailer parks sited near their nice little towns, relatively few of the trailers ended up being occupied—something like 19 percent, according to some estimates.

The other FEMA decision that had attracted a lot of criticism was putting people into hotels and on cruise ships. I know. Hotels? Cruise ships? Wasn't that going to be just a tad expensive? Well, yes, it was; just how expensive did not emerge until April of 2006, when an audit by the Department of Homeland Security's inspector general revealed that FEMA spent $632 million on hotel rooms alone. Six hundred and thirty two million dollars to house 10 of thousands of families at an average per family cost of $2,400 a month, which is roughly three times what FEMA later paid families to rent two-bedroom apartments.

And of course, the cruise ships cost even more. FEMA paid out $249 million to rent just over 8,000 cruise ship cabins for six months. DHS Inspector General Richard Skinner estimated that this worked out at around $5,100 per month per passenger—or six times the cost of renting a two-bedroom apartment.

While they were putting people into hotels and cruise ships, and trying to get them into trailer parks, FEMA was also looking to develop longer term solutions through programs that helped people enter permanent housing. One of the problems there was that instead of having one simple program that everyone could understand from reading a flyer, FEMA had three, which of course only added to the general confusion in the months following the storm.

Their tent pole program, the mainstay of what they were trying to achieve, was the Individual and Households Program, or IHP. This was used to provide rental assistance to about 490,000 households.

The IHP in fact channeled benefits awarded through two variant programs. The first, called the Standard Rental Assistance Program, provided benefits based on an inspector saying that your home was uninhabitable. The amount paid was based on the local Fair Market Rent, which is a figure determined by HUD.

If you qualified for the SRA, you got a check every two months while repairs were being carried out on your uninhabitable property. There was a cap on it set at $26,200 or 18 months' duration. So if you hadn't finished work on your house in that time, you were in trouble.

The second IHP variant was called the Transitional Rental Assistance Program, which was basically the same as the SRA but tweaked to meet the needs of Katrina evacuees. Under the TRAP (that's not what they call it, but I'm sorry, that's what the letters say), you didn't have to show an inspector your ruined house. If you were lucky enough to qualify for the TRAP, you got a check for three months instead of two, with the same cap as the other program, including the 18-month cutoff point.

In neither program could you use the FEMA benefits to pay for anything other than rent. If your landlord needed a down payment or security deposit, you had to find it yourself. On top of everything else, you had to prove you'd paid the rent with the money before the benefit was renewed for the next two or three-month period.

In addition to these rental assistance programs, FEMA used IHP to run the Other Needs Assistance Program. That could be used for home repairs not covered by a given individual's insurance policy, or for rebuilding a house destroyed by a disaster. Other Needs could also be used to pay for medical, dental, funeral, transportation, and moving and storage costs.

People who were getting benefits from either of the rental assistance programs could also apply for this assistance, but anything coming through the Other Needs Assistance Program was counted against the $26,200 cap.

It was all a little complicated and cumbersome, but that didn't stop people from making use of it. In fact, in the months following the disaster, around 900,000 households were approved for IHP assistance including 650,000 in the State of Louisiana, which accounted for $2.4 billion in support. But overall, the fragmented nature of FEMA support left people confused and frustrated.

Critics of FEMA said that they should replace the Katrina Disaster Housing Assistance Program, which was a temporary HUD program issuing vouchers to people who were already homeless before Katrina swept in, or were in some other way already HUD support recipients. They also called for the replacement of the FEMA-subsidized apartment program (which drew on federal subsidized housing stock) with what's known as the Section 8 voucher program.

Section 8 vouchers were used very effectively after the Northridge earthquake, which happened in California in 1996, although admittedly, that was a much smaller disaster. The 20,000 people made homeless there did not compare with the half million Katrina put out on the street in the Gulf Region. Similarly, the Northridge earthquake destroyed only 55,000 residential buildings, while Katrina devastated around 200,000.

But comparable or not, Northridge was a disaster. Like Katrina, it was sudden, and like Katrina, it left more people out on the street than there were places to go. And HUD's response to it worked.

Within a couple of days of the Northridge quake, Congress appropriated $200 million to support HUD in distributing

Section 8 housing vouchers that were good anywhere in California. Seven days after the quake, people were on the move, tens of thousands of families heading for apartments in what were often better neighborhoods than they had left behind.

HUD then followed up with a recruitment drive for landlords, encouraging them to take in quake victims. The process wasn't painless but it had clarity and momentum, and it gave people hope when they really needed it.

Apart from the issue of fragmentation, the big problem with the support FEMA was providing in New Orleans was that it left out the people in the middle. By that, I mean the people who weren't wealthy enough to just absorb the shock of the disaster and ride it out themselves, but who were not so economically disadvantaged as to have been former users of federal housing assistance.

The people in the middle never had help before, but they surely needed it then—and those people fell through the cracks. A lot of us thought that a Section 8 voucher program was exactly the right vehicle to meet their needs.

The other thing Section 8 vouchers had going for them was that there was no need to set up any new bureaucracy to handle applications or distribution. At the time of Katrina, HUD's Section 8 Housing Choice Voucher Program supported two million American families all over the country.

Yes, it was already up and running and drew on an existing network of housing agencies and private sector landlords—many of whom were located in areas already receiving families evacuated from the flood. And it was administered by housing experts with access to a huge network of apartment listings. These were people with hard won experience in counseling and placement, who could help families find rental apartments in the housing market.

FEMA was none of these things. Many of the families relying on the IHP and other FEMA programs were left on their own to find landlords who would accept rental assistance, and you can bet it wasn't always easy. One final thing Section 8 had going for it, and this was maybe most important of all, was that recipient families got 18 months of aid, no questions asked, whereas people drawing on IHP had to re-apply for assistance every three months, just adding to their anxiety.

But while FEMA was criticized for the piecemeal nature of its housing support, it was on the question of temporary housing that it really came under fire. There was this widespread feeling in the community that the building of big trailer parks was doomed to fail. People pointed to the fact that families who lived in the trailer park communities built after Hurricane Andrew were worse off than when they'd first arrived.

Trailer parks did nothing to help communities cohere or develop. On the contrary, they isolated people from jobs healthcare and each other.

Like most people, I always felt that mobile homes were at best a necessary stopgap that would allow workers and first responders to live close to where they needed to be. Trailers could also be very useful in allowing families to stay close to their damaged homes. In fact, a lot of people demanded that the trailer they'd applied for be sited on their land just so that they could stay close to their home, which more often than not meant staying close to their job, too—if they were lucky enough to have one.

After all, wasn't that the great thing about mobile homes? They were mobile. And as long as they weren't too big, they were perfect for a strategy based on targeted placement. And where it was impossible to get a trailer onto someone's land, people argued for putting them in parking lots, schools or even parks—anything rather than ship them out to some Greenfield site in the middle of nowhere and nothing.

Okay, I'm letting my passion show. And hey, it's easy to criticize; 20-20 hindsight is a wonderful thing. Suffice it to say that for whatever reason, FEMA took the road they took, and by the time we sat down with them to talk about the situation in the rental market, they were already on it.

CHAPTER SIX

The Cleansing

Whatever the FEMA people were thinking, as I said, back when we sat down to talk to them in November of 2005, they were committed to their different temporary fixes, and they were also committed to rehabilitating the residential areas.

They wanted our assessment of where we stood in terms of the housing stock. Our best estimate at that time was that there were about 210,000 homes damaged in the New Orleans region, with Plaquemines and Saint Bernard's Parish suffering the highest ratio of damaged property.

A survey of what was available on the rental front—and by "available," I mean viable and unoccupied—revealed approximately 45,000 units region-wide. Of that number, only 31,017 could be reached for survey and of those, 15,914, or more or less half, were damaged. So optimistically, we were looking at maybe 22,000 units of spare capacity. It didn't seem like an awful lot.

But, as I remember it, the FEMA people were pretty optimistic. By that time, the president had signed into law the Emergency Supplemental Appropriations Act to Meet Immediate Needs Arising From the Consequences of Hurricane Katrina 2005, which provided $10.5 billion in emergency funds to support FEMA and the Department of Defense. He had also signed the Second Emergency Appropriations Act of the same name, which provided $51.8 billion in emergency funds—$50 million of which was for FEMA alone, for "ongoing response and recovery."

I mean, with that kind of money being committed or promised or whatever the term was, how could we go wrong? Those appropriations gave everyone the feeling that the government was behind us, and that the money was soon going to be flowing in. There was, briefly, the feeling that everyone was on the same page.

Okay, Katrina itself had been a disaster, and maybe FEMA's response to it had not been optimal, but now they were going to put their shoulders to the wheel and use all that money to get things moving in the right direction. It was clear to me that they were under the impression we could get all our damaged units back on line pretty quickly.

The redevelopment strategy that came out of our meetings was two-pronged: we would expand the inventory of affordable, quality housing while at the same time stimulating local business. We wanted to get the region's social and economic heart beating again. Katrina had put New Orleans into a spin, a vicious downward spiral in which a sudden lack of housing meant an abrupt drop in population, which in turn meant an inadequate labor force, which was killing businesses, which meant fewer jobs, which meant fewer people and so on downward.

I remember the term "economic choke point" coming up a lot in those meetings.

We also talked about how important it was to rebuild the levee system in such a way that it could be depended on, which meant that it could be depended on even if a Category 5 hurricane swept in. Remember, when Katrina made landfall she was only a Category 3.

The restoration of the levees was obviously of critical importance because without a sense in the community and in the country that the levees could be relied on, the next time a hurricane came our way there would be no way businesses or families would ever return and reinvest. And that was what we all wanted. At least, that was what I thought we all wanted—to get people to come back.

I began to realize, as the months ticked by and the planning process got more and more bogged down, that getting the people back, returning the city to the way it was pre-Katrina, was not necessarily at the top of everyone's agenda.

In terms of specific policy, the decision was made to set up an administrative process that would facilitate the development of "temporary housing." In other words, things would keep moving the way FEMA had already been going since they first came into the region.

As I said in the previous chapter, trailers and variations on trailers were fundamental to their battle plan by that time, so I guess it wasn't surprising that our meetings with them came to the conclusions they did. I look back at the minutes of some of those early meetings and the trailer homes are right there, front and center: "Travel trailers should also be considered as an alternative for timely delivery and temporary housing—enough supply to meet short term needs in the Katrina-impacted areas."

Timely. Temporary. These were words that took on new meaning as the months rolled by.

In this temporary housing plan, preference was going to be given to employers and their employees, and then to first responders. The idea was to establish 30,000 homes, starting with 10,000 within six months.

The other side of FEMA's housing plan was going to focus on the "rapid rehabilitation" of damaged residential and rental stock. The thinking there was that just by repairing damaged stock, we were going to get 800 to 1,000 units back in inventory by late November of that year.

Once we had decided on the basic thrust of the strategy, the question was how to fund it—how to get all this money that the government was collecting on our behalf to fit within the city's requirements. To give FEMA credit, they saw very early on that the financing of repairs on houses and apartment buildings, and the securing of construction crews to do the work, was going to be a problem for a lot of people, including our owners.

We talked about different funding sources to provide bridge loan financing for owners who were either underinsured or had no insurance whatsoever.

There was some talk about the Small Business Administration loan program, but that capped off at $1.5 million and it was pretty obvious that amount would not get you very far with the rebuilding of a 200-unit complex. We tried to get the SBA to lift that cap for rental owners, but they said they couldn't help.

That's not to say that they couldn't help *anyone*. I understand that they have paid out (slowly, very slowly) $1.3 billion in disaster assistance loans to business owners and non-profit organizations, and more than $4.7 billion to renters and homeowners. But for the majority of my owners, they were no help at all.

So we thought about it some more and talked some more, and what came out of all that talk was a plan that came to be known as the Apartment Guarantee Program. Under it, FEMA would come in and basically guarantee payment of the rent of any given unit for 12 months. Owners who had insufficient insurance coverage could get an SBA or bank loan and then use the guaranteed income from the rent to start paying it off.

To us, it looked a workable system. Drawing on our databases, we produced a huge list of all our owners and handed it over to FEMA for them to start distributing it. GNO, Incorporated and AAGNO sent letters to all our owner members and then—well, I'm not sure what happened really, but basically, the scheme seemed to lose momentum. I do know that the response was not huge. One of the few complexes to take up the offer was Magnolia Garden Apartments, which had 117 units.

Certainly one of the reasons for the low uptake of the offer was that owners who were doing okay, who had tenant waiting lists a mile long, weren't really interested. For some reason they preferred to use their regular sources of funding. Maybe it was because part of the FEMA package was an obligation for owners to take more or less whoever FEMA sent them as tenants.

As you may know, landlords have criteria that each prospective resident must meet in order to rent an apartment. They like to be able to do a credit check and maybe find out about a person's rental history. Some owners even run criminal background checks.

At first, FEMA didn't want any kind of filter at all. They were more concerned with getting people off the streets and into decent housing. But after a while, they relented a little, allowing the landlords to carry out background checks for criminal records. But I think that by that time, a lot of our owners had found alternatives or had decided to go their own ways.

It was at that point that we started to put our focus on the East New Orleans area. It was a crucial turning point in the program.

Now, East New Orleans was and still is one of the hardest hit areas. The Lower 9th Ward, which is downriver of the Industrial Canal, was completely inundated and at one point was under about 10 feet of water, which then receded to about three or four feet and sat there for two weeks. So, as you can imagine, the mold that was left in those apartments and in the abandoned cars was just unbelievable, as was the challenge we faced in dealing with it.

East New Orleans was also an area of high crime and poverty. The unemployment rate in the Lower 9th hovered around 11 percent, 17 percent of households were receiving public assistance and half of them were single-parent. Around a third of the community lived below the official poverty line. Of course, all this was *before* the storm.

Prior to Katrina, FEMA had judged the Lower 9th to be low-risk because it was situated on slightly higher ground than some areas, and that meant that the banks offering mortgages didn't require people to buy flood insurance. That in turn meant that when Katrina flooded the area, a lot of owners were left with nothing, and without an insurance company's support, there was no way to rebuild.

Given all these different factors, maybe it's not surprising that the owners readiest to take up FEMA's offer of guaranteed rent came from this area. That's not to say that they were any more comfortable about having potentially unreliable or nonpaying tenants in their units—they weren't. Having only the criminal record check to orient them made them kind of nervous, too. And then, once they'd gotten their heads around taking more or less anyone, they had to deal with FEMA's notion of what constituted Fair Market Rent.

FEMA established a ceiling for what they were ready to pay based on numbers generated by Housing and Urban Development. Unfortunately, HUD's numbers were way off and by that, I mean way *below* the true market prices. To be fair, the prices were something of a moving target.

The situation in the city was evolving day to day. In July 2006, HUD released numbers showing that rents in the region had climbed by 39 percent since the storm. A 1-bedroom apartment that rented for $578 pre-Katrina later rented for closer to $800. So that was the curve we were riding, and it meant going back and forth with HUD to get them to raise their "fair market rates" so that FEMA could fix their rates accordingly.

And we did it. And we were all in agreement. So then we had a program, a delivery mechanism that looked like it could work, we had prices people could live with and we had owners who were willing to take the money on FEMA's terms. In other words, we had a plan. But you know what happens when you make plans…

Life happens.

Basically, we got hit by another storm, but not tropical this time. It was more of a social thing. It was in March, about two months after the plan had been put into effect that people from the East Side started to speak out against what FEMA was trying to do. A gentleman by the name of Sherman Copelin, the leader of the New Orleans East Business Association, stood up at a City Council Meeting and said that the Apartment Guarantee Program was going to put East New Orleans right back where it was before the storm, which in his view was not a happy place.

There was a fear that the plan might revive multi-family rental units like the Cindy Place Apartments, or Frenchman's Wharf and Patrick's Place, which were dotted along the Chef

Menteur Highway, Lake Forest Boulevard and the Interstate 10 Service Road. They were places that stood more or less derelict since Katrina.

What Mr. Copelin and other local residents like him wanted was to see those places disappear; to put it another way—to put it the way *they* put it—they wanted to "reduce density." And if the disappearance of those places was going to be part of that density reduction, no one was going to complain.

This all has to be seen in context, of course. There was a long history in the East Side of local people trying to limit the construction of multi-family rental units. In fact, as far back as 2002, local people had been protesting the spread of apartment complexes east of the Industrial Canal. They had even managed to put a stop to some multi-family dwelling projects that had been planned for what is known as District E.

At the beginning of 2005, the Katrina year, the local council approved a moratorium on permits for new construction or expansion of two family or multi-family dwellings. In other words, the social conditions and the attitudes were all in place for a big change of direction in the way New Orleans developed, long before Katrina came along.

Not that the local people were unsympathetic to the needs of those who had been left homeless by Katrina. It was just that they remembered the way many of the housing complexes had been run before the storm.

The Housing Authority of New Orleans (HANO), which was responsible for running 8,421 housing units in the city, 79 percent of which were nine very large "projects," had for a long time been a very troubled institution. In fact, the department of Housing and Urban Development had rated HANO one of the worst performing housing authorities in the country for more than 30 years.

The tenants in projects like Iberville and Florida had to put up with terrible living conditions, made worse by all the violent crime and drug dealing that was going on. At the time when Katrina rolled in, HANO was in the process of replacing some of its most notorious properties with better designed and better managed mixed income communities. HANO was also, by the way, pretty much bankrupt and under HUD receivership.

For people like Sherman Copelin, what Katrina had done was clean up a very unfortunate situation. Copelin and his neighbors wanted green spaces and new, vibrant commercial areas where the crime-ridden projects used to be. Simply put, Katrina had swept everything aside and when Mayor Ray Nagin, with his Bring New Orleans Back Commission, started inviting each neighborhood in the city to develop a plan for what it wanted to look like post-Katrina, people obliged.

The good people of New Orleans East even brought in an urban planning firm by the name of St. Martin Brown & Associates, who started working on their vision for a section of eastern New Orleans bordered by the Industrial Canal, Paris Road, Lake Pontchartrain and the Mississippi River-Gulf Outlet.

It was around that time, I think, that I first started to hear people say that "Katrina" was the Greek word for "cleansing."

CHAPTER SEVEN

The Long Road Home

It was also around that time, in mid-March 2006, that the Louisiana Recovery Authority, which had been set up by Governor Blanco back in October 2005, came out with its plan "to repair and rebuild quality housing in secure neighborhoods." It was called The Road Home Housing Programs, and for most of us in the Association—and I imagine it was the same for everyone in the city—it took its place alongside Mayor Nagin's various plans to do the same kind of thing.

Apart from wanting to establish a workable framework for the ongoing recovery effort, the underlying idea of Mayor Nagin and Governor Blanco's plans was to focus the community, to focus *the entire city* on the question of what exactly it wanted to be. Needless to say, it was a pretty tall order. The expression "herding cats" comes to mind.

The plans were in no way an attempt to replace what FEMA had been doing. They were supposed to complement FEMA's more nuts-and-bolts initiatives, which were designed—however flawed that design may have been—to address the immediate issues facing the city.

Of course, that begs the question, was it ever really going to be possible to separate the short-term initiatives from the long-term plans any given institution might have for the city?

Decisions made by FEMA in the immediate aftermath of the storm, particularly with regard to the buying of trailers and setting up of trailer parks, had implications for the way the recovery developed down the line. And as soon as FEMA did something that was clearly going to make a difference longer term, which was certainly the case with the Apartment Guarantee Program, the community that was going to be affected, *i.e.*, the people of New Orleans East, voiced their objections immediately. They started asking fundamental questions about where their piece of New Orleans should go next.

By mid-March, we were all asking those questions, partly because it wasn't clear where exactly we *were* headed, if anywhere at all. Six months after the storm, around 750,000 households were still "displaced," to use the official term. Six hundred fifty thousand households were getting rental support of around $800 a month.

Amazingly, the Army Corp of Engineers *had not demolished a single home.* Not because there weren't any candidates for the wrecking ball. There were. Driving to and from my work, I saw hundreds of shattered homes every day. According to official estimates, there were over 5,000 homes that needed to be pulled down in the Lower 9th ward alone!

And it wasn't because the Corps didn't have the manpower or the equipment. It was because they were caught up in negotiations with the "city leaders" about which homes should go.

On the new construction front, things weren't a whole lot better. Despite FEMA estimates that 50,000 homes in New Orleans had "major or severe" damage resulting from Katrina, only 16,000 building permits had been issued. Part of all this inertia derived from the fact that FEMA hadn't yet released its revised flood plain zones for the state. All the insurance contracts and bank loans that were going to have to be written were going to be based on those maps. Without them, everyone was pretty much in the dark.

But beyond that important technical issue, there was the bigger question of what the city or the state had in mind as far as bringing back any given neighborhood or parish. Because it was one thing to start rebuilding your house, but it was something else entirely to rebuild a sewage system that would let you flush your toilet. If the municipality didn't run a new drainage line into your section of town, you were in trouble. The same went for electricity or gas. You needed to know what their *plan* was.

We all needed a plan.

What we got were *plans*—different ideas from different consultants about what might be cool or neat or efficient.

It started back in November of the previous year, when Mayor Nagin brought in the first group of consultants from the Urban Land Institute. At first, it all looked quite promising. There were these gentleman—the ULI sent in a team of 50—who spent more than a month visiting the city to gather citizens' input and conduct research.

They then carried out an intensive, 1-week tour, during which they held a public forum—attended, it has to be said, by a fairly modest 300 people. They interviewed people representing—and here I'm quoting from the mayor's own PR—"a broad range of interests, including business, civic, political, cultural, utility, healthcare and education representatives and community activists."

They talked to all these people and devised their plan and then one of them stood up at a public hearing and said, "There are areas of the city that the panel believes should *not be* developed at this time."

Not developed? People sat up. It was the first hint of what was to come.

Nor was that the only thing the ULI people said that got people's attention. The gist of their plan was that we should rebuild, starting on the higher ground and then working our way down until we reached areas that were likely to get flooded again—and then stop. As for the lower areas, they needed to be turned over to parks or wetlands.

Well guess what? The people living in some of those lower lying areas didn't like it. They didn't like it at all. They were looking at generations of ownership and tradition being swept away by a planner's eraser.

Because remember—and this is something a lot of people don't realize when they talk about New Orleans—although the percentage of home ownership in the city as a whole was below the national average, a lot of people who did own homes had owned them for a long time. And in the poorer areas like the Lower 9th, home ownership was actually quite high at around 62 percent. People had lived in their beat up, shotgun-style houses literally for generations.

So you can imagine how those people felt when the consultant from out of town stood up to tell them that there were areas—and they *knew* he meant *their* areas—that should be allowed to just disappear under the grass.

Mayor Nagin, to his credit, had the sense not to be there when the people he had brought into the city revealed their plan. He told his office to say that he was doing something official in Washington, which also showed a lot of good sense given that he was actually on vacation in Jamaica.

So the mayor wasn't there. But Cynthia Willard Lewis was, a city council representative for New Orleans East who made it clear to all the reporters that she and her African American neighbors were not going to allow themselves "to be shoved into the back of the bus"—a reference to Rosa Parks and what that brave lady also refused to have done to her in the way of shoving.

The upshot of all this was that nobody took up the ULI's plan and it was allowed to get dusty in a corner. Meanwhile, Mayor Nagin started talking to the next set of consultants, this time a Philadelphia urban planning firm by the name of Wallace Roberts & Todd.

The head of the firm was a man by the name of John Beckman. What Beckman had going for him, apart from mad professor hair, was that he didn't need any "intensive week" of visits to study the problem or anything of that nature, because he had been working with the city since the 1970s and had in fact contributed to the creation of downtown New Orleans.

But familiar with the city or not, sensitive to local needs or not, Beckman's solution to the problem turned out to be pretty much like the one the ULI people proposed. What differed was his approach to selling it. None of that was surprising given that he came to pretty much the same conclusion the ULI team did.

The city's basic problem was one of size. Where there had been around 480,000 people before Katrina, there were, at the time Beckman was brought in at the end of 2005, barely 60,000. The people at ULI saw that and wanting to avoid mistakes that had been made in the past, most notably in Detroit, they said the city needed to "reduce its footprint." The city needed to be smaller and since that was the case, it made sense to withdraw from the places that were getting flooded.

When the French built the city, they stayed out of the marshes, and they were right to do so. And then we too needed to get out of the marshes and rebuild, probably at higher density, on the higher, dryer ground. Apart from anything else, the empty low-lying areas would be a perfect buffer and overspill zone during the inevitable recurrences of hurricane events. Any urban planner looking at a model of New Orleans would come to the same conclusion.

But that was the problem. New Orleans was not and is not an urban planner's model. It *is* a big complicated material thing with its sewers and streets, but it's also a living thing, with a living population—with all of the capacity for frustration and anger and resentment that a living population has. Beckman did nothing to change the debate, but he changed the procedure by which the city was going to reach its inevitable conclusions.

He said that the footprint of New Orleans should be determined by *the people of New Orleans*. It has a ring to it, doesn't it? A ring not unlike Governor Blanco's "no eviction for any reason"—a populist ring, a ring that any politician worth his salt could get behind, which is what the mayor did. So much so that this time, when a public hearing for Beckman's plan was scheduled in January, the mayor was actually in the room.

The ballroom at the Canal Street Sheraton, to be exact. The Sheraton was one of the first hotels to reopen after the storm, and to that extent, it was an obvious beacon of hope, a symbol of how our city could bounce back to its old sense of style.

As it turned out, the presentation never really got enough momentum for anything to bounce. When Beckman walked out onto the stage to give his presentation, he was confronted by a crowd of more than a thousand people, a lot of them standing and more or less all of them hostile.

In fact, in the days before the presentation, tensions had been running so high and the rumor mill had been turning so fast that the New Orleans City Council had voted unanimously to reject Beckman's plan, sight unseen.

For a while, it looked as though Beckman wouldn't even get to show his first slide. People were actually heckling him. To his credit, he grabbed the microphone and insisted that people pay attention. And to their credit, they did. In the end, he talked for almost an hour and by the time he started taking questions, the audience was ready to participate in a serious discussion—up to a point.

What Beckman's proposal came down to was a four-month ban on construction in the most heavily damaged areas. During the four months of the moratorium, the neighborhoods would be encouraged to organize meetings and discuss what they wanted for their areas. This sounds admirably democratic, but there was a sting in the tail.

By organizing meetings, the communities that made up the neighborhoods would be showing their vitality, showing that they were still viable. If any given community was *unable* to show that it was viable, well then…it would lose its property. That property would then be bought out by a new, as-yet-to-be-created "redevelopment authority."

What that redevelopment authority would do with the land was unclear. But I guess the idea was that once the people were out of the way, it would be possible to put together a plan unclouded by local community issues.

Now of course this plan raised some serious questions. For one thing, a lot of the communities were scattered all over the country, or at the very least all over Houston and Alabama. So how were they supposed to convene a meeting in, for example, the Lower 9th Ward?

Not surprisingly, people didn't like it any better than they'd liked the ULI proposal, and a number of local politicians were more than ready to give their dissatisfaction a voice and a focus.

Beckman had barely finished with his presentation when Marc Morial, formerly mayor of the city and then head of the National Urban League, denounced the plan. Jesse Jackson also weighed in, announcing that he was organizing bus protesters to fight Beckman's proposals.

As for Mayor Nagin, he said nothing on January 11th. A couple of days later, he appeared to give his support to the plan, saying only that it was going to need some tweaks, but after a week had gone by he'd changed his position completely. He said that for him, the paramount consideration was property rights. He told people to go ahead and build, and the city started issuing building permits that were briefly, incredibly easy to come by.

The next person to be brought in by the Bring New Orleans Back Commission was Reed Kroloff, the dean of Tulane University's architecture school. He and Ray Manning, a local architect, were mandated by the mayor to send out teams of professionals to help each of the city's 13 districts come up with their own neighborhood plans.

It was a little like Beckman's let-the-people-have-their-say scheme, but with the onus taken from the communities. In this case, it was the experts who'd be coaxing the plans out of the people, so they would nevertheless remain the people's plans.

The problem this time was that nobody could afford to pay Kroloff and Manning to do the work. The city had no money and FEMA, which was by that time picking up the tab for just about everything, refused to pay for yet another round of consultants. So Kroloff and Manning were obliged to step aside and watch as the city council set up its own commission, which in turned hired some *more* consultants, made up of—you guessed it—more architects and planners.

Having said that they had no money to pay Kroloff and Manning, the council then found $3 million, which they gave to the new team, telling them to get working on a plan for a new New Orleans.

This whole switchback ride of plan, proposal and rejection ran from October through February. Understandably, the city, by which I mean *everyone*, began to suffer planning fatigue. By February—that is to say, a month before the Louisiana Recovery Authority started really promoting its plan—any redevelopment momentum that existed was entirely uncoordinated.

Certain neighborhoods struck out on their own with no regard for the city or the state. Some people in the Bring New Orleans Back Commission still wanted Kroloff and Manning to show the way forward, arguing that those guys were the only ones with a plan for the whole city that had been put down on paper.

Then in March, six months after Katrina hit, the LRA came forward with its plan: The Road Home. What took them so long? The simple answer was that, like the mayor, Governor Blanco had been looking for a workable policy that would satisfy all the local parties. On top of that, because she stood at the interface of the state and federal government, she also had take into account the opinion of the administration.

In fact, in the aftermath of Katrina, the LRA had started out by backing a plan put together by Representative Richard Baker. The plan would have paid owners of flooded homes a minimum of 60 percent of their equity in the property. Assuming that gave the LRA title, they would then refurbish the viable units and afterward put them back into the market for sale.

It all made sense, but in January, the White House turned it down, saying that it didn't want to be in the real estate business. Needless to say, that angered a lot of people in the state.

But not everyone. One man kept a clear head. Sean Reilly, an LRA board member who had been state legislator at one time, went to meet with the federal coordinator for Gulf Coast rebuilding, a man by the name of Donald Powell. Reilly tracked him down to the town of Amarillo, and they went and had lunch together.

It was at lunch supposedly that they hashed out the housing recovery plan, literally scribbling numbers, categories and subcategories on a paper tablecloth. Of course, as always, it wasn't just about the numbers. Like the consultants Mayor Nagin had retained, Reilly and Powell were faced with ethical considerations that touched on the futures of various communities in the city.

An important part of Reilly's argument was the issue of federal responsibility. Having paid for the initial emergency response, the administration wanted then to direct its attention to the rehabilitation of the levee system. The White House had come to the view that it should support all the flooded homeowners who were outside the officially designated floodplain, and who had failed to insure themselves against flood because the federal government had stated that their area was not at risk.

Reilly took the view—and it was a view that the majority of people in New Orleans shared—that the government's liability went much further than that. People argued that the collapse of the levees was the responsibility of the government, insofar as they had mandated the Army Corps of Engineers to do the work; because of that, the government should pick up the tab for rebuilding and repairs.

It was an idea that was confirmed later on when researchers at UC Berkeley found that breaches due to design failings in the levees accounted for 80 percent of the water that flooded greater New Orleans. Without the structural failure of the levees, they argued, New Orleans would have been back to business as normal after a couple of months.

In fact, they said it would have been a question of a few wet carpets and damaged roof tiles, which is obviously an exaggeration; but anyway, their idea was that there would have been less damage. Reilly put this argument to Powell at their lunch in Amarillo, and although Powell was initially reluctant to accept it, later on he did just that.

Another set of consultants were brought in and working with the LRA and Powell, they put together a plan that Powell then presented to the president. Governor Blanco was brought into the discussions with White House officials who on February 15th announced that they would go to Congress for an additional $4.2 billion for rebuilding. Congress voted it through in June.

At that point, the city had—or supposedly had, because these things are never quite as simple as they seem—$10.4 billion that it could invest in rebuilding homes and businesses.

CHAPTER EIGHT

Social Engineering

The Road Home Housing Programs had a variety of objectives, but one of the central requirements was to get homeowners to return to the city; moreover, to return to the city and *stay*.

One of the worrying trends emerging through March and April was an increase in homes coming onto the market for sale. By May, there were over 3,400 private homes for sale in New Orleans, more than at any time since Katrina had made landfall, and up from the 2,800 that were on sale in February.

The trend held true across the entire metropolitan area except for St. James Parish, which for some reason remained relatively stable. To most, this increase in "for sale" signs was a signal that people were giving up on the city, turning their backs on it.

Just as worrying as the signs was the steadily shrinking labor force. In May, we were looking at a force that had shrunk every month since November. That was going on while just up the road in Mississippi, the labor force was back to its pre-Katrina levels.

Basically, New Orleans was slowly hemorrhaging people. The Road Home was in part an attempt to stop the bleeding.

Like a bookend to the principal of attracting home*owners* was the notion that lower income renters were also crucial to the city's continued vitality. The Road Home put a lot of emphasis on the importance of affordable rental housing and housing for "critical workforce." In a way, it was the biggest challenge facing the planners—how to provide accommodation that was affordable to a workforce that didn't make enough to pay market rates.

Like John Beckman's ill-fated plan, the Road Home wanted to ensure that neighborhoods were rebuilt based on "locally driven plans." That sounds like they were giving people a say, but it needed to be taken in the context of another driving principal in the Road Home, which was the promotion of neighborhoods that integrated mixed income groups.

As you can imagine, right there you had material for years of acrimonious debate. Not every well-off neighborhood wanted "poor people" in it, and there were plenty of "poor people" who wanted to go back to living where they'd been living before—maybe not in the best conditions, but happy in their sense of community and tradition.

Funding for the range of projects within the Road Home was to come from a "special appropriation" of Community Development Block Grant Program (CDBG) funds and from FEMA Hazard Mitigation Funds. Added to those two chunks was the $4.2 billion that the state was supposed to kick in, as mentioned at the end of the last chapter.

The program broke down into various carefully targeted segments starting with the Homeowner Assistance Program, which targeted owner-occupants and provided $7.5 billion in federal disaster recovery funds to help repair or rebuild homes, or buy owners replacement homes in designated areas. Homeowners also had the option of selling unwanted properties so they could be either redeveloped or given over to open space.

With a view to avoiding more flood losses in the future, all reconstruction work carried out was to be held to a high standard, meeting or exceeding the FEMA guidelines that were issued in April, which stated that buildings had to be least three feet "above grade" and three feet above the "base flood elevation."

Base flood elevation was the estimated height of a misleadingly called "100-year flood"—meaning a really bad flood of the sort that in the past had happened every century or so, but which, with climate change being what it is, might now be occurring more frequently.

Driving the whole program was the underlying desire to rebuild communities and make the city live again, not just provide compensation for losses. It was for this reason that the greatest financial and technical support was directed at the pre-Katrina and Rita homeowners, who committed to moving back to play a part in rebuilding southern Louisiana.

To be eligible for Homeowner Assistance, an owner had to have been living in the damaged property as a primary residence at the time of the hurricanes, and the home had to be in a single-unit structure. There were other provisions for multi-family structures, which I'll get to in a moment.

Also, to get aid, the owner needed to have registered for FEMA Individual Assistance and needed to have had the home categorized by FEMA as either "destroyed" or having suffered "major" damage.

For owners who had received Small Business Administration Loans to make repairs to the structure, the amount of the grant was adjusted by a formula that took into account the value of the SBA interest rate discount; but whatever the numbers, and their were plenty of them, and they were plenty confusing, the ceiling on assistance for owner-occupants was $150,000. That was the figure everyone could recite, and the figure they clung to.

Homeowners who were in a position to do so were required to contribute whatever insurance payments they had received to cover structural damage, as well as any FEMA payments they might have received, toward the cost of repairs or replacement. The basic idea was the provision of assistance tailored to homeowners' losses: someone who suffered 50 percent damage to his or her home wasn't going to receive as much assistance as an owner with 80 percent damage. Obviously.

The Road Home also took into account whether or not a home was inside the FEMA flood zones, and whether it had been insured at the time of the storms. Despite Reilly's arguments about federal liability, people who had lived in a flood zone without insurance *were* penalized.

They were still eligible to receive up to the $150,000 ceiling on the same affordable terms as other homeowners, but they were given more responsibility for repaying the assistance than their neighbors who, in the words of the Road Home documentation, "followed prudent practices for homes in flood zones and bought flood insurance."

As mentioned above, the other cornerstone of the Road Home program was support for the establishment of affordable rental housing. Here, the LRA's stated goal was that affordable rental housing should be made available to displaced residents of "all" income levels who wanted to rent. In other words, even if you made beds in one of the city's many hotels and you got minimum wage, you were entitled to a place to live.

This aspect of the Road Home was based on the assumption that it was the rental housing stock that was going to support much of the workforce essential to the city's economic recovery. Just as we at the Association had determined in our meetings with FEMA back in November, the LRA had come to the conclusion that without a workforce, we didn't have a city, and without affordable housing, we didn't have a workforce.

You wanted to avoid above all what some people have called the "Aspen Syndrome," named after the famous ski town. Aspen Syndrome kicked in when you made your town so expensive that the "help" shipped out, leaving the millionaires to collect the garbage in their snowshoes. All politics aside, the simple fact is that capitalism needs a little help sometimes. It's called social engineering.

The Road Home also took account of the fact that before Katrina, a lot of very low-income working families lived in single-family homes, but also in "doubles" and small, multi-family buildings that were owned and operated by small-scale landlords. As it turned out, a lot of those properties were either underinsured or completely uninsured.

To help the landlords out in these cases, the LRA proposed what they decided to call "gap financing," the main purpose of which was to fund the cost of repairs and limit the amount of debt owners had to carry. Not because that was just a nice thing to do, but to *enable them to charge affordable rents*.

The program offered funding up to $25,000 to restore a rental unit that was going to be renting at market rates, but higher levels of funding for landlords who committed to charging lower rents for a period of 10 years, *and* accepted low-income tenants. The amount of block grant financing available rose to a ceiling of $75,000 per unit, with the higher financing available to owners who agreed to offer the lowest rents.

The financial assistance on offer took the form of a deferred payment mortgage at zero percent interest, which only came due when the property was sold, or when an owner failed to respect the restrictions on rents and the incomes of people he was supposed to be renting to.

When it came to the repair or replacement of multi-unit buildings occupied by the owners, the LRA decided that it was unfair to be provide financial assistance to, say, 20 rental units in a given building at as high a level as for the owner-occupied unit—that is to say, up to $150,000 per unit.

Similarly, the LRA was worried that if the owner-occupant in a multi-unit building wanted to sell, payment of the pre-storm value to the owner of the rental units would be too much for the state to bear. For those reasons, such mixed occupancy structures were eligible only for the Homeowner Assistance Program, which capped at $150,000.

To fund the programs, the LRA introduced the Low-Income Housing Tax Credit (LIHTC) or "Piggyback" Program, under which Congress had authorized tax incentives of around $1.7 billion over three years that would facilitate investment in the repair and construction of affordable rental housing. By combining the resources of the LIHTC tax incentives, block grants and private investments, the LRA hoped to get 25,000 new or restored rental units up and running, 10,000 of which would be rented at market rates and 15,000 *below* market rental rates.

Again, there was a strong element of social engineering here, which had as its goal not just the restoration of the rental housing stock, but the creation of new, mixed income communities that would bring Louisiana's workforce back home.

Not surprisingly, the social engineering aspect of the program attracted some criticism. Generally speaking, people got the idea that you needed a workforce to run a city, but there was grumbling about the middle class being left out and fears that the wrong kind of people were being encouraged to come in.

Representative Steve Scalise, for example, argued that the affordable rent program was nothing more than a Section 8 program by another name. Section 8 is federal housing assistance for people on low or no incomes, which doesn't sound so bad unless you happen to think that this is the kind of program that attracts a certain kind of welfare-dependent population, which then becomes one more burden for the city to bear.

This became a big issue in the summer, when Jefferson Parish Councilman Chris Roberts proposed that landlords be obliged to hire around-the-clock security if they were accepting federal housing subsidies for 20 percent of a building occupied by eight to 20 families; 15 percent in a building occupied by 21 to 60 families; or 10 percent in a building occupied by 61 or more families.

Councilman Roberts had come to the view based on monthly rides with sheriff's deputies and what he referred to as "routine monitoring" of incident reports. He'd concluded that there was a direct correlation between high crime statistics and apartments that the government was, to use his phrase, "giving away for free." His idea was that heightened security at those complexes would lower the incidence of crime in the parish, and it was a position that got the full support of the local police.

Deputy Chiefs Newell Norman and Craig Taffaro of the Jefferson Parish Sheriff's Office said that the larger apartment complexes, where it wasn't uncommon for 10 people to cram into a one-bedroom unit, were crime hot spots. These were places where people were being shot at.

Now, we at the Association were very much in sympathy with the residents who felt threatened, and we were certainly not blind to the fact that New Orleans does have a crime problem.

In fact, since the 1980s, the city's homicide rate has consistently ranked in the top 5 of large cities in the country—along with Detroit, St Louis, Atlanta and Louisville.

And along the way, we have even been able to set a few records—like in 1994, when 421 people were killed, a ratio of 85.8 per 100,000 citizens. That homicide rate remains unmatched by any major U.S. city, although the good people of Detroit came close in 1999, with 415 killings.

Not only do we have a lot of violent crime, but ours tends to be concentrated in certain, specific neighborhoods—and yes, these neighborhoods are often characterized by a high density of public housing and particularly by large housing projects. Our murders tend also to be concentrated in what I guess you'd have to call the criminal class, with most victims of homicide being killed within three months of their last arrest.

Add to all that the fact that violent crime dropped significantly post-Katrina, and you start to get the kind of picture that invites the kind of views expressed by Deputies Norman and Taffaro.

But there are ways of dealing with crime that help, and ways that don't. As far as what Councilman Roberts was suggesting, apart from the obvious issue that his proposal would tend to stigmatize all people on welfare as criminals, it seemed to us that there was every likelihood that the demands the councilman was making on landlords would just encourage those landlords to stop accepting federal vouchers.

This, in turn, would mean that low-income residents would be forced into the larger complexes that were able to pay for security details and voila, you'd be back to the kind of concentration of poverty that was perceived to be such a problem before Katrina.

The other problem was the cost of hiring an around-the-clock security guard or "courtesy officer," as we prefer to call them; I estimated that it would cost the owner of the building something like $130,000 a year. Where was the owner supposed to get that money? Certainly, one place he'd be tempted to go would be his tenants, whom he would simply charge a higher rent. It was all very unsatisfactory, and in the end, the plan was dropped.

Meanwhile, the LRA's Andy Kopplin kept stressing that the gap financing initiative was really a workforce housing program, and he kept on talking about how the city needed a workforce until finally the program got approval from the legislature in September.

At that point, $869 million was committed to small rental property repairs, a grant geared toward landlords with one or two units. To qualify for what was termed a "forgivable loan," a landlord had to keep rents down to between 50 percent and 80 percent of the area's median income, which in post-Katrina New Orleans for a family of four was $52,300.

Finally, the state recognized that the city was going to need new developments across the full range of housing types, and so it put together a plan to encourage developers to build in the New Orleans metropolitan areas and other communities that had suffered major losses to their housing stock.

A total of $75 million was budgeted for incentives of this kind. The Housing Development Loan Fund provided "seed funding"—early commitments of capital to incentivize developers to build mixed income housing in the communities that lost the most housing. Loans would be directed to both nonprofit and for profit developers of new rental and single-family housing that was affordable to families with incomes below the area median. There would be a strong preference for well-designed residential communities and infill housing developments.

Generally speaking, the response to the LRA's initiatives has been neutral to favorable, with most criticism directed at the glacial slowness with which funds have been disbursed. The Road Home was fully funded and ready to go in July, but by mid-September, it had paid out only a staggering $1 million of the $10.4 billion it had allocated to support home and apartment owners.

Inevitably, people made comparisons with the recovery plan implemented by Governor Haley Barbour in Mississippi. Under that plan, the state took the insured value of the home in question, multiplied that number by the damage (expressed as a percentage) that the home had sustained, subtracted any insurance or FEMA payments that might have been made and then wrote a check up to a maximum of $150,000.

Once the owner got the check, he could use the money for whatever he wanted, and stay or leave as he chose. The only obligation he had was to settle up with his bank any outstanding mortgage liability.

By comparison, the LRA's delivery mechanism was more complex. First, there was the issue of larger grants being provided to people who decided to rebuild *in situ*, or at the very least buy a home somewhere in the state. Second, the LRA program required the establishment of escrow or disbursement accounts, which had to be monitored by mortgage lenders and closing agents whose job it was to make sure the money was spent on approved rebuilding, or on a home in Louisiana.

All this created red tape, which required bureaucracy, which required, as we all know, time. ICF International, the company administering the Road Home program, now forecasts that it will take five to seven months just to *process* all the applicants—which means, of course, that some people will live in uncertainty until March 2007, 18 months after Katrina came through.

As someone pointed out to me recently, at the current rate of disbursement, it's going to take the LRA 100 years to hand over all the money—making it a very long road home for us all.

A Post–Katrina Survival Guide

But in a way, the glacial pace of disbursement is the least of our problems. Because, despite all the talk and all the "planning," the city still lacks a clear direction. It's one thing to say that this money is available for you to rebuild your house; if you don't know whether the city has a plan to bring your neighborhood back, you're still going to wait before you start banging in nails.

The latest attempt to develop an overarching vision of what the city should become got started in July. The so-called Unified New Orleans Neighborhood Plan, which included all 73 of the city's neighborhoods, not just those damaged by Katrina, was financed to the tune of $3.5 billion by the Rockefeller Foundation and was managed by a nonprofit created for the purpose.

Apart from the money, the Unified plan has strong support from the LRA; in fact, it was New Orleans businessman David Voelker, an LRA board member, who first outlined the *new* new plan at a meeting of the LRA. The meeting was held at Jackson Barracks, yet another symbolic place, chosen, like the Canal Street Sheraton, to show how the city could come back.

Jackson Barracks is a military base that dates back to the 1830s and is currently the headquarters of the Louisiana National Guard. The 100-acre base was badly flooded by Katrina and is going to be rebuilt under a $200 million plan, which will serve as a model for the rest of the city; part of the project includes a charter school, a health clinic and a library and media center.

Conscious of everyone's growing impatience with the seemingly endless planning process, Voelker set himself a kind of deadline, saying that residents would have a much clearer idea about the prospects for the various sectors of the city by December. He then warned everyone that the plan was "a work in progress"—which I guess was a way of saying. "Don't expect too much by December."

The Unified plan brought together Mayor Ray Nagin and certain city council members, who supposedly put aside their differences and decided to work together. As I said, it had the full support of the LRA, but it still faced the intractable issue of which neighborhoods could be brought back, and which should be let go.

And of course, like every plan the city has so far generated, this one has its detractors, the harshest critics saying that the city is betting its future development on a ragtag agglomeration of neighborhoods that are fraught with racial tension and distrust.

A Miami-based urban planner and housing consultant by the name of Paul Lambert, who was hired by the New Orleans City Council to come up with a plan for the city's worst-damaged neighborhoods, has been publicly critical of the Unified plan process, which he says has actually delayed the release of federal recovery aid to the city.

Meanwhile, Councilwoman Cynthia Willard-Lewis, the lady who didn't want to be shoved to the back of the bus, has made references to the "malaise of planning" in which the city seems to be stuck. Cory Turner, a fair-housing and criminal justice activist, has complained about the Unified plan's failure to unify, saying that six months from now, the city will be no further forward, still arguing about plans.

CHAPTER NINE

The Big Difficult

More than a year has passed since Katrina came through this city, and we're still feeling the effects of her rage. At the end of September, only half of New Orleans' pre-Katrina population of 454,000 has returned, and housing still remains in short supply.

For some, the city will never be the same again; for some, New Orleans will, at best, be reduced to something like a Creole theme park with a port. This devastated place that we used to call the Big Easy.

Of course, in the struggles of the past year or so, New Orleans has revealed itself to be anything but easy, and if FEMA has shown itself guilty of a certain amount of incompetence, it's also true that we haven't done everything we could have to improve our situation. The net result has been a recovery characterized by glacial slowness and endless debate.

Not that progress hasn't been made. It goes without saying that reconstruction has been easiest and quickest in the areas least damaged by the flooding. These areas mostly correspond to the parts of the city developed before the 1900s—areas that were built on the higher ground along the riverfront. Old Carrollton, Uptown, the Old Warehouse District, the French Quarter, Old Marigny and Bywater were minimally affected by the storm, as were the areas built along natural ridges, such as Bayou St. John and Gentilly Ridge.

Most of these places were either completely unaffected by the flooding or suffered only moderately due to the raised design of the older architecture. As I said at the beginning of the book, before engineers like A. Baldwin Wood got hold of the town, the people of New Orleans expected to get their feet wet once in a while and built their houses accordingly. Older houses in Bayou St. John don't let the water in; it's as simple as that.

The Lake Shore developments between Lake Pontchartrain and Robert E. Lee Boulevard, which are built at a higher elevation than nearby land, also escaped serious flooding. Where the levees held, as was the case in the West Bank section of the city, reconstruction has also progressed rapidly.

Algiers, for example, which was spared flooding altogether, was one of the first parts of the city to reopen officially to residents. In neighboring Jefferson Parish, the West Bank communities suffered only a little wind damage and some flooding caused by torrential rain. Parts of Metairie and other Jefferson communities located on the East Bank did experience some flooding, but because the levees held there, it was much less serious than the flooding experienced across the parish line in Orleans.

A Post–Katrina Survival Guide

The real problem areas for New Orleans have been those neighborhoods that suffered not just flooding but Katrina's storm surge, the bow wave she drove before her that was channeled into the city by the Mississippi River Gulf Outlet. The storm surge slammed into New Orleans East and parts of the 9th Ward, and of course most catastrophically the Lower 9th Ward, located below the Industrial Canal. Similarly deluged were Saint Bernard and Plaquemines Parish.

So that's the first thing you notice about the recovery: it's going forward best in the areas where the going is easy. Elsewhere, progress is patchy at best. Gas and electricity have been almost completely restored to the whole city, although there are still power outages. The Army Corp of Engineers has dragged away most of the estimated 300,000 rotting refrigerators from people's front yards and alleyways and streets; ditto the quarter million wrecked cars. Since July, most of the city has had postal service.

As of mid-October, safe drinking water, the most basic of public services, flowed throughout the city; the last place to get it was the northern section of the Lower 9th Ward. Apart from anything else, it will enable the residents there to put FEMA trailers on their property, something that's been impossible until now because FEMA won't install a trailer without there being potable water available.

Next, the residents will turn their attention to getting Entergy New Orleans to put the power back on in the six-by-nine-block section of the Lower 9th, west of the Industrial Canal. As for reopening the Lower 9th Ward campus of Dr. Martin Luther King, Jr. Charter School for Science and Technology, which has been operating at a Central City site this semester, that struggle is ongoing.

But the last section of the city without drinking water now has it. And so another milestone passes...

Meanwhile, the Army Corps of Engineers completed a first "provisional" rehabilitation of the city's levee and pump system in June, and we are now *supposedly* a little safer than we were before Katrina. Apparently, the water from Lake Pontchartrain will no longer be able to surge into the 17th Street Canal in the event of another storm swell.

If I sound a little skeptical about all this, it's because as of mid-October, the exact nature of the levee system that the Army will eventually deliver is still undecided. And the same goes for other hurricane protection structures.

The Corps is due to present its plan for Category 5 hurricane protection for Congressional perusal by December—at which point Congress will be looking at more funding needs, more bills, more appropriations…

Meanwhile, a recent independent review of the 6,000-page interim report commissioned by the U.S. Army Corps of Engineers on the flooding caused by Katrina in New Orleans, carried out by the National Academy of Engineering and the National Research Council, stated that engineers have not been entirely candid about the risks involved in living here. The independent review also said that the Corps needed to do a better job of setting out the parameters for what it would take to build a system that would *guarantee* protection in the event of future Katrina-scale storms.

Ed Link, an engineer with the University of Maryland who is leading the Corps' ongoing study of the levee problem, recently said that they were still gathering data on storm surge, wave heights and other factors that go into quantifying exactly how risky it is to live here. In other words, over a year after the storm, they still don't know.

Apart from being more than a little worrying for the people living here, this is also a major source of frustration for anyone trying to develop a plan—a fact that was pointed out in the

National Academy of Engineering review, which said that the public is hoping the Corps will provide "a basis for resettlement decisions" for New Orleans and the region.

Too true. In the absence of solid information about how safe any given area is going to be in the event that another major storm strikes, developers, residents, and city and state officials are unable to make decisions about what to do with areas that were flooded. So, for the time being, we struggle on in the dark, and despite whatever small improvements have been made here, the overwhelming sense is of a city marking time.

The clearest indicator of this is the fact (and this is amazing to me) that only half of what was promised to the city in the form of federal aid has actually been paid out. *Half.* People in the community are frustrated; my *owners* are frustrated. They find it hard to understand how it is that after four emergency spending bills committing a total over $110 billion in aid, only $44 billion has actually been disbursed.

It's a situation that has provoked outrage on all sides. Louisiana Senator Landrieu called it like it was when she said that the recovery has been handled no better than the original response to the disaster. Amy Liu, deputy director of the Metropolitan Policy Program at the Brookings Institution, described FEMA's efforts as "the most cumbersome, reflexively slow response we've ever seen when it comes to disaster assistance."

Reed Kroloff, the architecture dean at Tulane University who worked on one of the early rebuilding plans for the mayor's office, is even more scathing, calling post-Katrina planning "the perfect storm of bad policy."

The perfect storm. There's an irony in that somewhere. Mr. Kroloff is also on record as saying, "If you wanted to kill a city, this was the way to do it"—by letting it drift, by avoiding the difficult issues, by failing to face the underlying realities.

But is New Orleans dead?

Not yet. Not by any means. It'd take another couple of storms like Katrina to finish it off and even then, there'd be something here. Of course, some people, maybe even a lot of people, think there shouldn't be anything here at all. They think we're crazy to live in this partly-below-sea-level city and deserve everything we get, just like those nutty people who choose to live on the San Andreas Fault in California.

But I would gently remind those people that when New Orleans was founded, the site was chosen because of its relative *elevation*. It wasn't until much later that we wanted to start pumping the water out and allow the city to spread beyond the higher ground, natural river levees and bayous, into the low-lying areas. And it was only over the course of the 20th century that natural and human-induced subsidence left those newly populated areas several feet below sea level, and the erosion of the coastal wetlands exposed us to the full weight of incoming storms.

New Orleans had always been vulnerable to flooding, but it was only well into the 20th century that people began to understand how vulnerable the city really was.

All of which is a way of saying that the situation we find ourselves in, which has developed over a couple of centuries, *is not all our fault*. And look at the Dutch! A great deal of their finest real estate only exists because of artificial dykes. So it is by no means beyond the capabilities of mankind to protect this city.

And it should be protected. For one thing, New Orleans is important to the culture of this great land of ours. That is not just a proud resident speaking from her heart (which it is, and I am), but it is something borne out every year by the millions of people who come here as tourists.

New Orleans is one of the most visited cities in the United States, with approximately 14 million tourist to view the architecture, taste our food or listen to our music. We have some of the best food anywhere—etouffée, jambalaya, gumbo, po'boy and Italian muffaletta sandwiches, Gulf oysters on the half shell, beignets...

There's also the city's world-famous carnival, which goes by the name (and I probably don't even have to tell you this) of Mardi Gras, or "Fat Tuesday." It centers on the French Quarter, drawing enormous crowds. In addition, we have the Sugar Bowl, the New Orleans Jazz and Heritage Festival, and the Voodoo Fest. There is also (if you like that kind of thing) Southern Decadence—one of the biggest gay and lesbian celebrations in the world.

But even if you forget about the cultural heritage and the sheer sassy, dark, magical vibrancy of the place, just from the point of view of the city's two ports—which are, by tonnage, the nation's biggest—you would have to have something here.

We handle roughly a third of the nation's seafood and more than a quarter of its oil and natural gas. Around 4,000 oil and natural gas platforms, connected by 33,000 miles of pipeline, spread out like a network of veins along the Louisiana coast, feeding among other things the 17 petroleum refineries here, including the four largest in the Western hemisphere.

People working in the local petroleum industry will tell you proudly that southern Louisiana is as important to the nation's energy supply as the Persian Gulf. Not surprisingly, the state is also home to two of the country's four Strategic Petroleum Reserve facilities.

The simple fact is that New Orleans is sited slap-bang on top of an arterial trade route that existed even before we settled here. The city is built on trade, just like all the big cities in the U.S., and so the Big Easy isn't going anywhere.

Maybe it will never die, but it could go into a decline, and that's what a lot of people fear: that it will shrink and wither as people become discouraged and move away. Already the city is hemorrhaging the kind of professional people we can't really afford to lose. Nearly half the medical and three-quarters of the psychiatric doctors have left, for example; teachers, too, are moving away.

Of course, one way to stop that from happening is to build decent, affordable homes like the complex that's going to replace the Houma House Apartments, behind East Jefferson General Hospital, which are slated for demolition in October.

The Houma House Apartments were flooded by about two feet of water during Katrina, and the apartments on the first floors of the five-building complex were gutted in the aftermath. But such was the demand for housing, right up until the complex was sold to the developers in July (for $9.25 million), that there were people still living on the upper floors.

The five-acre site is surrounded by nearly a dozen private medical facilities and the units, which will be sold as condos, will be marketed primarily toward healthcare workers and priced between $179,000 and $300,000. That means that if all the units sell, the property will be worth in the region of $60 to $65 million.

Significantly, the new development, which is to be called Metairie Palms, will be built to the new, stricter building code, which includes 130 mile per hour wind-resistant windows. Also, to guard against future floods, part of the complex, a 4-story building containing 152 units, will be built on top of 10-foot concrete pillars.

There will also be a natural gas backup generator to run refrigerators and freezers in the units during electrical blackouts. That's right—that was one lesson we learned, and learned well from Katrina: whatever else you do, make sure the refrigerators keep working!

Another conversion is going on at what used to be a 200-unit apartment complex between the Houma House and the hospital. The Camelot, as it is called, is being converted into condominiums by Patrician Management of Baton Rouge and the units, which range in size from 800 to 1,000 square feet, are apparently selling at $147 per square foot.

Local people watching these apartment-to-condo conversions worry about the effect they're going to have on the rental market, but if it means keeping the city's hospitals staffed with competent professionals, it's hard not to see it as a price worth paying.

Another more controversial initiative to bring professionals back is the LRA's offering of 250 modular units to public school teachers. So far, union officials have tended to dismiss the units, saying that they are no better than storage pods—suited for furniture, maybe, but not human beings.

In fact, a posting on an American Federation of Teachers Website says, "New Orleans offers storage pod to teachers!" But the LRA describe them as "two-bedroom, fully furnished, rent-free modular units." According to Ramsey Green, the LRA's education policy director, the units are fully equipped and even include things like pots and pans.

The whole project will cost $14 million, which works at about $56,000 per unit; that sounds pretty expensive until you compare it to the $75,000 FEMA pays for each of its trailers. Importantly, the modular units can withstand winds of up to 185 miles per hour, *i.e.*, the kind of winds produced by a Category 5 hurricane.

That is definitely not the case with the 18,383 FEMA trailers currently sited in New Orleans. They have to be evacuated even in a lowly tropical storm, which generates winds of only 74 miles per hour.

Of course, like every other initiative taken in the city, this one comes with its political baggage. Here, the back story is that many of the 7,000 teachers and employees who worked in the New Orleans public school system pre-Katrina are still angry about the decision taken in November of last year to put the majority of them out of their jobs.

School officials argue—and it's hard not to see their point—that the destruction of our stock of school buildings and the virtual disappearance of the majority of the student body meant that keeping all the teachers on payroll just made no sense. But for many in the unions, the legislature's decision to place 107 of 128 public schools into the state-run Recovery School District, which is not subject to union rules, was opportunistic.

So into all this ill-will and distrust come these "pods"; whether they are going to cut it, or whether we can build enough complexes like the Metairie Palms to bring back qualified medical staff, remains to be seen. In the meantime, the city is still losing professionals.

As for the trailers—those famous trailers, which were going to be part of the "temporary solution" to the immediate Katrina crisis—FEMA was supposed to be getting rid of them by February of 2007, which would mark the 18-month deadline set for FEMA relief by the Robert T. Stafford Disaster and Emergency Relief Act. But now, apparently, they are going to be around for a while longer, in recognition of the simple fact that the recovery effort is going so slowly that it is highly unlikely there will be enough housing in February for people to go to.

As of September, FEMA estimated that there were 298,000 people still living in trailers on the Gulf Coast, while there are just under 60,000 trailers in the New Orleans region. Several thousand people are still on waiting lists, hoping to get one eventually.

Trailer parks of various sizes are scattered over the landscape from here to Baton Rouge. With the recent announcement that the February deadline will not be respected, FEMA enters new territory in which it has to balance the comfort of the people living in the trailers against the city's need to get them back into the regular housing market.

Not that living in these places is a picnic. At the Renaissance Village, for example, a 62-acre grid of gravel and grass that is home to roughly 1,500 people occupying 437 trailers (another 136 are empty), there are plenty of people who would love to get out.

Do the math and you seem to be looking at around 3½ people per trailer, but it's not unusual to find families of 6 or even 8 in a single 80 by 30 foot box, the only upside of which is the air conditioning. And while that probably sounds like a luxury item to a lot of people, I can assure you that down here on one of our hotter, more humid days, AC is an absolute necessity.

The Renaissance Village trailer park—FEMA prefers the term "group site"—is located 90 miles northwest of New Orleans, a short drive from Baton Rouge and near a town call Baker. There's a run-down strip mall there, which is where the people from the trailer park go to get their groceries.

It was the residents of the trailer park who chose the name back in October of last year. "Renaissance" is of course French for "rebirth"—a hopeful name for people who were ready to make a new start. In the immediate aftermath of Katrina, living in a trailer looked a whole lot better than some football stadium or abandoned airstrip, and of course, most people thought that they were only going to be there for a short time anyway.

But that is not the way it has turned out. The number of people living in trailers declined by 5,000 from the high point in June, but as one group of people leaves, another arrives. As of September, there were 132 trailer parks still operating in

Louisiana and roughly 8,000 displaced people still waiting to get in. Some FEMA officials think that going past the February deadline is the least of it; some people believe that the trailer parks might have to be supported for the foreseeable future.

The problem is that not only did Katrina drive people out of their homes, she also destroyed the homes they left, severely damaging more than half of the homes in New Orleans—especially affordable ones. More than a year later, the city has 80 percent fewer public housing units than it did pre-Katrina, and the rents in the units that are left have risen by as much as 25 percent.

In a way, this is the real problem the people in the trailers face—not the lack of available housing, but the lack of housing they can afford. For all the reasons given in this book, the economy of the city has changed in the past year.

So until things change pretty radically, a lot of these people are stuck, and a lot of them are afraid because the crime that existed in the city exists in the trailer parks too, and trailers are less secure than houses. Private security officers patrol the Renaissance Village's gravel roads in golf carts, but few people feel safe.

Beyond that, they are isolated. Children have to travel miles to school. A bus service ferries residents lacking cars to a nearby bus stop, but the trailer park is where it is—in the middle of nowhere, rural East Baton Rouge Parish.

All that said, the one big thing the Renaissance Village has going for it, apart from air conditioning, is the fact that it is free. Water and electricity is paid for, and there is no rent. The only thing people have to buy is the propane to fire up their stoves.

Now, however hard it might be for people, not paying rent or utilities can be a big incentive to stick around. And the longer people do stay, the more they will get to know their neighbors and the more acceptable it may seem to be. This is what FEMA worries about most—people settling in, people settling down. This is why they send around teams to check up on people, asking them what they're doing to find housing.

But at the same time, there's a growing acceptance—especially now that the 18-month deadline has been abandoned—that this is the way things are going to be for a while, and with that acceptance has come a relaxation in the rules.

FEMA has already begun to relax restrictions on what can and can't be built on-site inside their various trailer parks. At the 450-trailer Diamond Group site, which is in Plaquemines Parish, FEMA is now allowing local charities, working in conjunction with Save the Children, to open a community center that will include childcare and other social services, as well as a play areas for kids.

If all goes well at the Diamond site, the charities intend to expand their services to other trailer parks, with as many as 10 community centers getting up and running by next fall, and further out, up to 20.

FEMA has some experience in maintaining trailer parks long-term—some of the parks in Florida, for example, have been up and running for over two years. But there's a sense that what is happening and what is *going* to happen in Louisiana is somewhat of an experiment.

All this is temporary, of course, and what the city really needs is for the Road Home money to start to flow, and by that I mean *really* flow. The city also needs to get working on the rehabilitation of public housing stock.

Residents of the city's public housing developments have grown increasingly critical of the stop-start nature of attempts to reopen the bigger complexes, but officials with the Housing Authority of New Orleans claim to be on target to open 1,000 apartments in the three months running up to the holidays. This includes units in the Fischer and Guste complexes, as well as in the Iberville and B.W. Cooper complexes.

So is the city dying or is it being reborn? Sometimes it seems like it's just a question of what you look at—whether you want to see a glass half full or half empty; whether you want to focus on the devastation in the Lower 9th or the transformation that is taking place in areas like Lakeview.

According to data provided by the city's Department of Safety and Permits, Lakeview, a neighborhood of some 7,000 homes traversed by Canal Boulevard, has at least 1,400 houses slated for demolition. As of mid-October, just under 600 have already been torn down, a number far larger than you'll see anywhere else in New Orleans.

In some cases, the teardowns are happening in response to the city's new anti-blight enforcement program. Elsewhere, it's people wanting to forget the misery that Katrina brought, wanting to make a clean start.

But there are other forces at work, too—more optimistic forces that are hard not to read as a return to the community's old vitality. There's genuine excitement in Lakeview among residents who are tearing down older, relatively modest properties in order to build on a grander scale. On Vicksburg Street, for example, older, split-level homes are disappearing and being replaced by imposing, three-story properties offering up 3,300 square feet. A lot of people have been buying half of the next-door lots, which they are splitting with the neighbors on the other side.

As elsewhere in the city, reconstruction is hampered by owners having to search far and wide for a homeowners insurance policy at a rate that isn't going to ruin them. Similarly, people are having to wait for resolutions to financial issues, the most important of which being the question of how much of a rebuilding grant the Road Home program will provide.

That said, according to developers, most of Lakeview's demolition work is being driven by insurance and private money, and that is why it is pushing ahead the way it is. Also, there is the knowledge that with all the work done on the levees, the neighborhood is unlikely to get flooded again.

The transformation of Lakeview is happening so rapidly that conservationists are afraid the area is about to lose the quaint, cottage-style living that has characterized the traditionally middle-class neighborhood for the past 50 years; post-World War II cottages and split-level homes make up the bulk of Lakeview's housing stock.

Hoping to save as much of that character as possible, the Preservation Resource Center is offering Lakeview owners case studies that show renovation to be typically much less expensive than new construction. Similarly, they are keen to point out that south Lakeview, with its Arts and Crafts bungalows that date back to the 1920s, is home to a National Register historic district.

The LRA is also alert to the dangers of how a redevelopment boom could fundamentally alter the city. In July, they published a 92-page manual titled, "Louisiana Speaks: Pattern Book," which contains drawings, photographs and advice about how to go about building storm-resistant homes that will retain a south Louisiana look and blend in with the patina of adjacent older homes.

So far, around 90,000 of the books have been distributed, the bulk of them through the Lowe's Home Improvement Store chain. The book can also be viewed on the Louisianaspeaks.org Website, which I recommend, by the way, to anyone who wants to get a handle on developments in the housing sector in New Orleans.

Despite its efforts to guide the community in its redevelopment choices, the LRA isn't looking to establish any formal design regulation. The main reason for this is that whatever the concerns about the city losing its character, they are vastly outweighed by concerns about the city losing its population.

Before Katrina, Lakeview had a population of more than 20,000. How many are left is hard to say, but a recent survey noted that only 20 percent of its lots had occupied homes or FEMA trailers. Another 22 percent of residential lots were under construction. It'll be a while before this lovely neighborhood is back to its old self.

Whatever direction the rebuilding of Lakeview takes, it is hard not to see all the activity as positive for the people who have decided to stay put. And, of course, Lakeview is not the only place where the wrecking ball has started to swing. Gentilly is another neighborhood that looks to be undergoing rapid transformation, with city records showing 714 demolition permits granted there and 174 homes already demolished.

On the basis of demolition permits granted, it looks like the Lower 9th is also going to be making a comeback. Government officials or homeowners there have already secured close to 1,000 demolition permits. The wrecking ball has yet to start really swinging, however, with just 24 homes of that 1,000 having actually been torn down, according to the most recent city records.

Similarly indicative of coming change are the nearly 1,300 homes in the Lower and Upper 9th Wards that are classified as being in "imminent danger"; these homes will be torn down using federal dollars. In Lakeview, also, hundreds of residents have put themselves down on a list of nearly 1,700 homeowners citywide requesting that the federal government tear their houses down.

So is the city being destroyed or transformed? Is the glass half empty or half full?

Keeping a positive outlook certainly helps me get through the day. In the right frame of mind, even some bad things can show a more promising side; even FEMA, for example.

Yes, even FEMA got it right sometimes! Some aspects of their recovery effort did actually work—the flood insurance program, for example, is widely recognized as having done the job it was designed to do.

Before Katrina and Rita swept through, 385,000 Louisiana homes and businesses had flood insurance policies. The cover ran at about $140,000 for average premiums, around $450. Something like half of the insured properties were damaged in the storms, and FEMA has so far paid out just over $13.2 billion under the National Flood Insurance Program (NFIP), meeting average claims that ran at around $70,000.

Since the hurricanes, another 43,000 NFIP policies have been written in the state, with an average coverage of $170,000.

Other agencies did less well. They were either overwhelmed by the enormity of the challenge or just too rigid to do away with all the red tape. One of the worst offenders in this regard was the Small Business Administration.

The SBA was singled out by the Government Accountability Office in a report it produced in July, which said that the recovery loans they'd issued had been held up by "significant delays." And here, as always, it's one thing to talk about delays in the abstract; it's another to deal with people trying to cope on a daily basis because the long awaited check just isn't coming through.

I know of a gentleman living in Lakeview, for example, who applied for an SBA loan 1 month after the storm surge pushed water over the levee and flooded his house. He had 10 months of looking out at what used to be a great neighborhood, but which Katrina reduced to a semi-ghost town with debris-strewn lots and vacant houses. He had 10 months of not knowing if he'd ever be able to pay the half a million dollars it was going to take to rebuild his lovely house.

His problem—and it was a problem shared by a lot of people—was that his insurance just didn't cover the damage. The company finally paid out just $20,000. So he went to the Small Business Administration, whose job it is to offer loans for homes and businesses damaged in natural disasters. He went to them just after the storm, and in November of 2005, he was told that the SBA could offer a $250,000 loan. The only problem was that it took 10 months for them to pay.

And of course, he's not alone. A report produced by the Democratic Party's House Small Business Committee revealed that of the $10 billion approved by the SBA, only 20 percent had reached the entitled parties. So I guess there are a lot of people still waiting.

Naturally enough, it would have been a big help to know by, say, December 2005 what was going on with SBA disbursements. But that has been one of the big problems overall regarding the recovery: it's been impossible to get a handle on how any given aspect is going. Every time you see a number, it seems to contradict the number you saw the day before.

And this isn't just me getting confused about the numbers. A report produced by the Brookings Institution in August, which looked at federal distribution of funds, starts with the sentence, "Federal allocations in response to hurricanes Katrina, Wilma and Rita now total $109 billion. Additionally, over $8 billion in tax relief is available. While these numbers appear quite large, widespread uncertainty exists over how much of this money has been spent and where."

Now, if someone at the Brookings Institution whose job it is to pick through balance sheets and statistics can't figure out what's going on, what chance do the rest of us have? This is important because, however tedious it might seem to have to find out what's really going on, if you don't know what's been spent (and I mean spent as opposed to "committed," "allocated" or "earmarked," or any other of the weasel words officials have used as code for "not yet spent"), you have no way of knowing what kind of progress is being made or how effective any given agency is being.

It wasn't until August 2006, one year after the storm, that the White House Office of Management and Budget released an agency-wide breakdown of recovery spending. Why was that? I'd hate to think that it was because they didn't want people, and by people I mean *voters*, getting a sense of what a mess the recovery effort was in. I only say that because when the Office of Management and Budget finally did release the numbers, they weren't exactly encouraging.

They showed, for example, that the Department of Housing and Urban Development had "committed" $11.5 billion in block grants, mostly through housing reconstruction programs administered by Louisiana and Mississippi, but had spent only $100 million of the overall *$17.1 billion* Congressional allocation.

That's right. HUD spent—*i.e.*, forked out, paid up, handed over—$100 million out of a possible $17.1 billion.

Staggering.

The money just didn't come through or wasn't pushed through soon enough and that simple fact was largely to blame for the late start in rehabilitating the city. It's not a matter of politics but a matter of record that the administration's first request for Katrina aid, in October 2005, included only $1.5 billion in HUD block grants. It was a *token*, a Band-aid for an amputee.

And by the time the real money started to flow, six months had gone by, momentum had been lost and all the arguments about which way the city should go had been given ample time to fester. Similarly, Louisiana's $10.2 billion in federal housing obligations were not "secured," as the expression goes, until mid-June because of all the arguments going on between state and federal officials about how housing money should be distributed.

Since then, more than 100,000 homeowners have applied

for HUD-originated grants under the Road Home program, and applications continue to pour in at a rate of 2,000 a day. A good percentage of the owner-occupiers that the LRA made their number 1 priority seem to be coming back.

There are an estimated 123,000 homeowners eligible for the $7.5 billion in aid under the Road Home program, and fully 54 percent of the first group of Louisiana homeowners to apply wants to rebuild rather than take the money and move to another state. Eleven percent wants to take the money to buy elsewhere within the state, and only one percent has elected to clear out altogether.

The remaining 30 percent or so is undecided about what exactly to do and is probably waiting, like so many of us, to see exactly what is going to happen before making a commitment.

And guess how many families have actually received any money? At the end of September, the figure stood at a mind boggling 190. But that's changing, apparently. The latest delays have been due to red tape,—that and the complexity of administering the grants. In the next couple of months, thousands of homeowners in Mississippi and Louisiana are set to receive hundreds of millions of dollars in government grants to pay for rebuilding, and a new phase of the recovery will begin.

The scramble for contractors is going to get ugly. That's why the Louisiana legislature set aside $15 million to train construction workers. The U.S. Department of Labor also put up $10 million in grants for Mississippi and Louisiana community colleges to give free classes in basic construction skills. Similarly, a Washington-based association of CEOs called the Business Roundtable has committed $5 million to recruit and train 20,000 new construction workers by the end of 2009.

Whether these well-meaning initiatives are going to be enough is another question. In New Orleans alone, the forecasted demand for construction workers ranges from 30,000 to 100,000. And with unemployment in the area running at around 3 percent, it's going to be hard for the construction industry to find the manpower.

But, as was the case after Katrina, Hispanic workers are expected to fill many of the breaches. According to a recent study by Tulane University and UC Berkeley researchers, one-quarter of the workers in New Orleans post-Katrina are undocumented Latinos, and the construction boom that is about to start will be sustained by their hands.

And of course, housing is going to be a critical issue, just as it has been since Katrina. You can draw construction workers into the city, but where do they sleep?

CHAPTER TEN

Lessons Learned...

There have been times in the past 14 months when I have felt like I was on the steepest of learning curves as a mother and a wife, but also as a representative for the Apartment Association of Greater New Orleans, a person owners come to for explanations and advice.

Certainly, walking through the flood-damaged remains of the Hickory Creek apartments was one of those times; or there was the time I had to explain to my owners that the governor wouldn't allow them to clear their units of waterlogged furniture until they got permission from their missing tenants.

I learned some lessons in those situations. We at the Association put some of them into a kind of guide for our owners, which you can find on our Website. Most of it is common sense, but you'd be surprised how resistant people are to doing the simplest things, simply because they never think the bad stuff is going to happen to them.

One of the simplest things you can do as an owner is get in touch with your residents at the beginning of the hurricane season. Just send out a form if that's the simplest thing to do and ask that, in the event of a hurricane or tropical storm, they take some precautionary steps, starting with removing any items from their patios or balconies and putting them inside their apartments.

I know, it sounds too obvious. But people don't do it, and abandoned exercise bicycles and surfboards have ways of being sucked off balconies in hurricanes, and becoming lethal projectiles. So, it's better if they are *inside*.

Also, tell your residents to fill tubs with water in order to be able to flush toilets should the area lose its water supply. Above all, tell residents to clean out their refrigerators before evacuating.

Unless you as an owner have had to deal with blocked toilets and maggot-filled fridges, the importance of each of these items will probably not have registered sufficiently. So just take a moment to think, and tell yourself that you are going to print up some nice clear instructions and have them ready to hand out the next time storm season comes around.

You should also recommend that all residents purchase renters and flood insurance for their personal items, because the property insurance will not cover such things.

As for the aftermath of a hurricane, it was our experience that communication was the biggest issue. It's amazing what a major storm can do to a city's phone lines. I was lucky during Katrina in that I was able to use my cell phone pretty much the whole time, but remember, cell phones depend on transmitters to work and most of them can be blown down just the same as an ordinary telephone pole.

The best line of defense is the Internet. If your company has a Website, use it to post regular updates and make sure residents know how to get to it. HRI used its Website as the principal means of communication with both employees and residents in the aftermath of Katrina. There are, of course, plenty of people who never go online, but at least if they know that your company has a Website, they can get someone—even if it is just a friendly librarian—to guide them to it.

If you don't have a Website, you should probably think about getting one because hey—this is the 21st century for one thing, but also because the minimal outlay in cash and brainpower will be more than repaid the next time you find yourself in the middle of a Category 5 storm.

Non-technophobes who can afford it might also want to look into available satellite telephone services. Direct Way and Hughes Satellite Service provide super high-speed Internet service and can also feed Vonage phone service adaptor boxes, which emulate standard telephone lines. Net2Phone service (www.net2phone.com) can also be used with a laptop for making outgoing calls wherever Internet connectivity is available.

Making sure that residents can get in touch with you is of course important, but just as important, or maybe even more so, is making sure that you can reach them. This was one of the biggest headaches my owners had after Katrina—not being able to call people because the phone numbers they had on their lists were either inaccurate or out of date.

So, you need to make sure that you have up to date phone records. The same is true, of course, of your staff, because without them, you are, as the saying goes, on your own.

Here again, the Internet is your best friend. At HRI, most of the 70 employees fled the city and scattered across Texas and up the east coast. The only information available to them regarding conditions in the city, other than HRI's regularly updated Website, was television news. In other words, without the Web, they would have been in the dark.

As far as dealing with the recovery, that is a more complex issue and depends to a large extent on the relationship you have with your insurance company, and what sort of deal you have with contractors.

On the insurance side—and here I'm talking about the basic issue of getting your insurer to pay up—it seems that there is no way around it being a horrible experience. I've heard it again and again, across the whole gamut of owners: if the insurance company can settle for less than they really owe, they'll do it. And the only way to counter this is by being sure of the details and being incredibly persistent.

One of the more interesting facts to come out of New Orleans in the past year or so is that claimants living in white neighborhoods have been three times as likely as homeowners in black neighborhoods to go to the state to get help in resolving insurance disputes. People paying attention to this issue say it proves that lower income people of color are disconnected from the government institutions that could help them, or just actively distrustful of anyone in power.

Well, maybe it does show that, but I would argue that it also shows that if you don't do everything possible to get an equitable settlement, including going to the state, you won't get one.

According to Associated Press research, to date, of the more than 700,000 insurance claims filed for damage resulting from Katrina in Gulf Coast states, only $14.9 billion out of $25.3 billion in insured losses has been paid. In other words, the insurance companies are holding onto roughly $10 billion that doesn't really belong to them.

In Louisiana, more than 8,000 residents have filed Katrina-related complaints with the state insurance office. AP got a look at the dossiers of more than 3,000 complaints that

A Post–Katrina Survival Guide

have already been settled and analyzed the outcomes by the demographics of the victims' current ZIP Codes.

Nearly 75 percent of the settled cases were filed by residents currently living in predominantly white neighborhoods. Just 25 percent were filed by households in predominantly minority ZIP Codes.

It appears that income was also a factor. The average resident who sought state help lives in a neighborhood with a median household income of $39,709, compared with the statewide median of $32,566 in the 2000 Census. But the distinguishing feature was the extent to which the white claimants went to the state for help and got it.

One of the most common complaints among my owners, coming second only to complaints about insurance companies not paying enough or not paying on time, was the lack of contractors to affect vital repairs. For larger companies like HRI, getting contractors to do what they say they would do was a big problem, and they ended up hiring a major national disaster recovery firm that was able to provide contractors and subcontractors on demand.

HRI has said that the next time there is a Katrina-equivalent event, they will go straight to the big national firms simply because local contractors are either overwhelmed or dealing with their own disaster situations.

So these are the lessons I have learned in my job at the Apartment Association.

But what about as a citizen? What about as a member of the community? Certainly, I've been faced with circumstances that seemed to offer lessons and certainly, I've tried to learn. But of course, I'm just a member of the community, not the community itself; and for things to improve, I think the community as a whole needs to understand some things. The community as a whole needs to act in concert, as they say—in agreement.

But looking at the way we have responded so far, you have to wonder about our capacity ever to do that. You have to wonder about our capacity, collectively, to learn. If there is one thing Katrina reminded us, it was how susceptible our city is to flooding; and to a *man*, the planners told us to get back to the dry ground, to keep out of the flood plain, just as the French did when they first built this city.

But did we learn that lesson? Not according to the evidence. Not if you consider the fact that nearly three-quarters of the people who've applied for LRA grants so far say they're going to rebuild their homes in areas that were flooded during Katrina. Maybe they think that new city rules about raising homes by at least three feet are going to make a difference the next time the levees fail.

Or maybe they think that obligatory federal flood insurance is going to be sufficient to cover them if it rains too hard—the federal flood insurance program that collected $2.2 billion in premiums last year, but which will have to pay out the estimated $20 billion in Katrina claims, leaving taxpayers to pick up the $18 billion difference.

It's a thing like this that makes the rest of the country despair, and it's a despair I understand. People get a little frustrated at the thought that their federal tax dollars will not only be paying for reconstruction in flood areas, but also underwriting insurance on the new homes. They'll also probably be bailing out the flood insurance program once the homes get wiped out again and it becomes clear that the insurance program doesn't have enough money to pay.

People also worry that by offering insurance at reasonable rates in areas where private insurers won't go, the program actually encourages people to build in areas that are likely to flood. Of course, this applies nationwide and not just in New

Orleans. But wherever it is happening, the inevitable outcome is more costly disasters for the taxpayer to support.

As for the three-foot rule, which was adopted by the New Orleans City Council on September 1st, I would argue that all it does is create a false sense of security while imposing an unnecessary burden on the people who don't need to raise their houses. The extra yard of elevation is pointless in areas that didn't flood after Katrina and is totally inadequate for places that saw the floodwaters reach heights of 20 feet!

Katrina had plenty of other lessons for us and reminded us particularly of the different ways in which our city didn't really work—socially and economically. America was shocked to see the people wading out of the floods, shocked by the depth of their poverty, and to a woman, the planners told us we had to rebuild our city in ways that did not concentrate poverty or cut people off from the city's basic services.

The planners told us we had to squeeze up a little, build a little tighter, a little denser. Pre-Katrina, one-quarter of the population did not own cars. To the extent that one-quarter traveled at all, they took public transportation. The planners told us that if we wanted public transportation we could afford, we needed to squeeze up a little; if we wanted utilities we could afford, we needed to squeeze up a little; if we wanted safe streets policed in sufficient numbers, we needed to squeeze up a little.

That for me has been one of the big lessons we didn't learn—that as a city, we need to reduce our footprint.

You only have to look at the way the city is coming back, *growing* back, particularly in the east, to know that this crucial lesson has not been learned. A number of large apartment complexes are scheduled for renovation. In and of itself, this is kind of amazing. You only have to drive out there and look at the wrecked houses and the abandoned cars and the uncollected trash, and listen to the silence, to see how hard it's going to be to bring those neighborhoods back. But even so, people are rebuilding.

According to some local brokers who specialize in the multi-family real estate market, as many as 4,000 of the 7,000 units that existed pre-Katrina are slated to eventually come back on line. For some, this is a good thing, a sign of the sheer determination of the community to get back on its feet.

But to others, it's a disaster, symptomatic of our abandonment of every plan drawn up in the months following the storm. People want what back what they used to have and don't see why they should give it up.

And somehow, this attitude has dovetailed with the Road Home program's emphasis on the building of affordable rental units and the commitment to retaining a workforce, to create a kind of plan without a plan—a dynamic that will push money into areas where the city as a whole probably can't afford to go.

The danger in allowing uncoordinated redevelopment to take place is that it could eventually lead to something the urban planners always hold up as a worst case for New Orleans—a situation in which the city is characterized by jack-o-lantern neighborhoods, great areas of darkness, lawlessness and substandard services, dotted with single houses or single apartment complexes.

Not that all of the apartment buildings are coming back. Some landmarks have already fallen. The 384-unit Walnut Square complex, for example, which was located next to the Interstate 10 service road near Crowder Boulevard, has already gone. The 644-unit Frenchman's Wharf and 520-unit La Provence Apartments look as though they might be next for the wrecking ball. The future of the Georgetown Apartments looks similarly bleak.

The Housing Authority of New Orleans, whose plans I talked about in the last chapter, are being joined in their efforts to revive East New Orleans by private investors, many of them from out of town. These people are drawn by the possibility—and you have to admire their drive and optimism—of doing business here. These are people like the Los Angeles-based Champion Group, which is renovating the 584-unit Chenault Creek complex, a property Champion acquired three years ago.

Champion wants to break down the 30-building, 18-acre complex into separate neighborhoods, the idea being to reduce the oppressive feeling urban density and provide open spaces for children to play in.

Open spaces! Children! Such optimism!

Of course, it's going to cost money to achieve this vision, and the cost will inevitably be passed on to the tenants in the form of rents which are likely to be as high as $1 per foot—some of the highest East New Orleans has ever seen.

Triangle Realty is another out-of-town company, a North Carolina native that first got into New Orleans real estate five years ago by buying into the 216-unit Copper Creek apartment complex. Triangle purchased the 400-unit Wind Run Apartments off Bullard Avenue (yes, the very place we visited with the National Apartment Association when they came to town, the place that was so badly flooded) and the 350-unit Lakewind East complex. The company intends to renovate both.

Copper Creek was one of the first complexes to be renovated after Katrina. Inevitably, given the demand for housing in this city, the complex is now fully occupied with rents running about 85 cents per square foot, which is on average $100 more expensive than before the storm.

A one-bedroom unit on the second or third floor of Copper Creek runs about $625 per month. On the first floor, units have been completely refitted with new appliances and rent for $695. It's the market rate, but still affordable for the kinds of working families, waiters, teachers and retail outlet employees that Triangle wants to attract.

While things must look pretty rosy for Triangle Realty at the moment, it's going to get harder in the year to come, as units come on line through the Louisiana Housing Finance Agency's low-income housing tax credit program. Complexes such as the 200-unit Gaslight Square Apartments and the 408-unit Willowbrook Apartments, both of which are Housing Finance Agency complexes, are going to have the backing of the Gulf Opportunity Zone Act.

This act has implemented a "bonus" first-year, 50 percent depreciation for landlords and other developers within the program. These people can write off half of the cost of any given project in the year the project is completed.

There are all these signs of life, but still no sign of a plan.

Not surprisingly, John Beckman has been among those speaking out against the way the city seems to be headed, arguing that it was a big mistake to reject his plan for a more compact urban fabric. Similarly, Reed Kroloff still argues for a more compact city, explaining that this doesn't have to mean a *lesser* city or even a city with a smaller population. As he points out, before World War II, New Orleans was 40 percent smaller in surface area with the same population it had before Katrina.

Other voices have been added to throng. Ken Topping, an expert on disaster recovery and formerly the planning director for Los Angeles, who was in Kobe, Japan, after the 1995 earthquake, is absolutely convinced that New Orleans needs to get its overall plan straight before breaking it down by neighborhood. The city needs to focus on fundamental issues like affordable levee protection before talking about affordable housing.

That didn't happen. We never got that overarching plan. And so now, life is just happening, just as it did when Katrina first decided to come calling on us. If ever New Orleans is going to become that denser, more vibrant city that the planners and many of the rest of still hope it can be, it needs to be led there. But who's going to lead us?